# PERFECT DAY
# KENTUCKY

Day Trips, Weekend Getaways, and Other Escapes

Library of Congress Control Number: 2024930401
ISBN: 9781681064857

Printed in the United States of America
24 25 26 27 28   5 4 3 2 1

Title page images *(left to right)*:
1. Rough River Dam State Resort Park (Courtesy of Kentucky State Parks)
2. World Chicken Festival, Corbin (Courtesy of World Chicken Festival)
3. Tousey House Tavern on the B-Line®, Burlington (Courtesy of meetNKY)
4. Abraham Lincoln Birthplace National Historic Park Memorial Building (Courtesy of NPS Photo)
5. Eiffel Tower, Paris (Courtesy of Paris-Bourbon County Tourism Commission)
6. Red River Gorgeous Tradewinds Tree House (Courtesy of Tina Brouwer)
7. Downtown Campbellsville (Courtesy of Taylor County Tourist Commission)
8. Yuko-en on the Elkhorn (Courtesy of Georgetown/Scott County Tourism)

Table of Contents page images *(left to right)*:
1. Downtown Bowling Green (Courtesy of VisitBGKY)
2. Rail Explorers, Versailles (Courtesy of Scott Carney/Rail Explorers)
3. Murray/Callaway County Quilt Trail (Courtesy of Murray, Kentucky, Convention & Visitors Bureau)
4. Abraham Lincoln look-alikes, Lincoln Day Parade, Hodgenville (Courtesy of Pam Spaulding)
5. Bison at Big Bone Lick State Historic Site, Union (Courtesy of Dawn Garvan)
6. Gallery of Dummies at Vent Haven (Courtesy of Kathryn Witt)
7. Background image: Horse Cave KOA Holiday (Courtesy of Kathryn Witt)

# Dedication

To my sister Karan—and many more adventures.

Kentucky State Capitol, Frankfort
(Courtesy of Julie Hill/Frankfort
Tourist Commission)

# PERFECT DAY
# KENTUCKY

Day Trips, Weekend Getaways, and Other Escapes

**Kathryn Witt**

# Contents

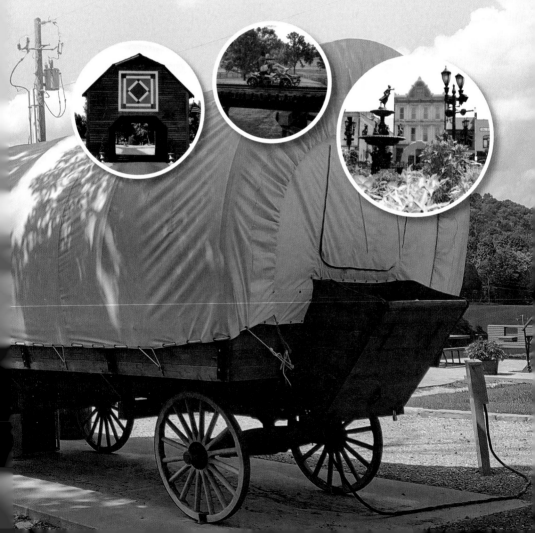

Van Hook Falls, Daniel Boone National Forest
(Courtesy of Greg Davis/Kentucky Wildlands)

# Acknowledgments

Among the many wonderful characteristics about people who work in travel and tourism is their passion for what they do—and for good reason. They're in the business of discovery, exploration, adventure, and fun. They know about the latest museum exhibition and restaurant opening, the newest and most extraordinary overnight lodgings, the best fishing hole, coolest coffeehouse, and most scenic trail for optimal waterfall and fall foliage viewing.

They are also very generous with their time. So when I sat down to write about all the outstanding experiences in Kentucky, I knew I would need their expert guidance to narrow down the possibilities for a perfect Kentucky day (and there are endless options!) to the quintessential experiences.

Much appreciation goes to Kathy Yount, director of marketing at the Kentucky Department of Tourism, who graciously provided thoughtful insights. Your input was invaluable in planning and organizing the book. To Kristina Wooldridge, director of communications, thank you for searching for and sending the perfect photos.

If national parks are "America's best idea," state parks surely run a close second, and Kentucky's state parks have a reputation for being part of one of the country's finest park systems. To LaDonna Miller, director of marketing and sales at the Kentucky State Parks, I appreciate your feedback about the various state parks; and to Dawn Garvan, also with the Kentucky State Parks, thank you for fulfilling my many image requests.

To all my friends in Kentucky Tourism who answered questions and shared thoughts and photos about their destinations, thank you. And to Georgetown/Scott County Tourism and Old Friends Thoroughbred Retirement Farm, special thanks for facilitating a photoshoot for the book's cover photo.

The wonderful thing about Kentucky is, no matter how many times you visit, there is always something new to see and experience—so many ways to create a perfect day.

Evan Williams Bourbon Experience,
Louisville (Courtesy of Kentucky Tourism)

# Introduction

Birthplace of Abraham Lincoln, bourbon, bluegrass music, and beer cheese—with a whole delicious experience, Winchester's Beer Cheese Trail, devoted to this culinary delicacy . . .

Home of the longest known cave system in the world at Mammoth Cave; the "Niagara of the South" at Cumberland Falls; the country's largest private collection of original 19th-century buildings at Shaker Village of Pleasant Hill; the country's most intact Civil War battlefield at Perryville; the world's longest underground suspension bridge at Hidden River Cave . . .

Bourbon Capital of the World (Bardstown), Horse Capital of the World (Lexington), Houseboat Capital of the World (Lake Cumberland), Bar-B-Q Capital of the World (Owensboro), Quilt Capital of the World (Paducah), Batter Capital of the World—yes, batter—(Hopkinsville) . . .

Among "state capitals"—the Country Music Capital of Kentucky (Renfro Valley), Folk Arts & Crafts Capital (Berea), Covered Bridge Capital (Fleming County), Zip Line Capital (Cave City), Farm Tour Capital (Oldham County), Outdoor Adventure Capital (Horse Cave), and State Capital (Frankfort) . . .

UNESCO Creative City (Paducah), Kentucky's largest old-growth forest (Blanton), coolest car—the Corvette—(seen at Bowling Green's National Corvette Museum), and "the most exciting two minutes in sports" at Churchill Downs and the Kentucky Derby . . .

A home where the bison roam (elk, too), dinosaurs lumber, a family of happy-go-lucky giants camp and another family, immortalized in stone, marches onward but never moves, and hundreds upon hundreds of dummies communicate but seldom speak . . .

Visitors to the Bluegrass State find all this and So. Much. More. Aboveground and below, and around every bend in the road.

Kentucky was made for perfect days. And perfect days are always at home in Kentucky.

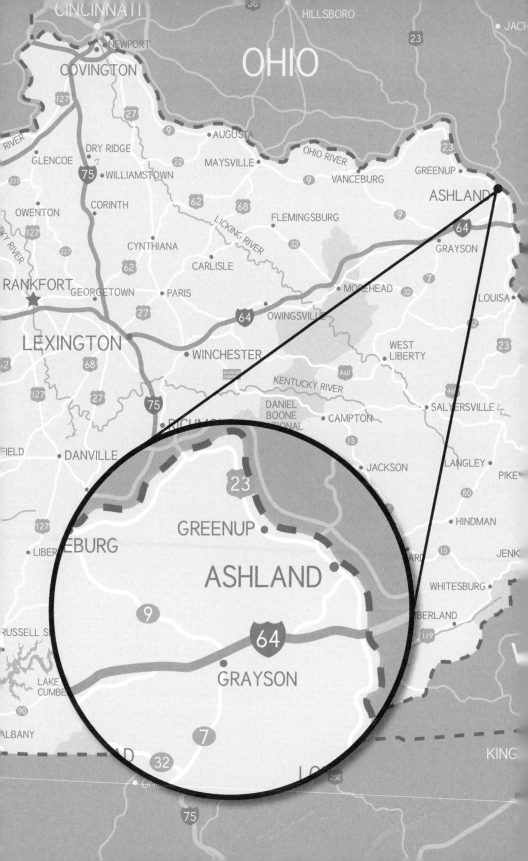

# ASHLAND

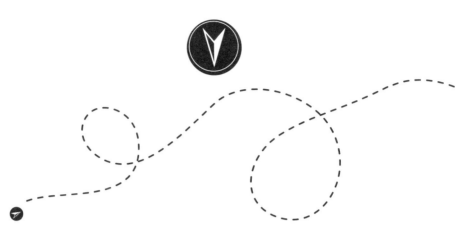

**A** BEAUTIFUL RIVERFRONT, a lush park with fountain and gardens, Indian mounds, over 1,100 trees, a walkable downtown vibrant with color and seasonal blooms—all this and more greet visitors to Ashland.

Temptation awaits at locally owned shops and restaurants while outdoor art beckons—from extraordinary art installations to the flood wall murals next to the Ashland Train Depot that dip into the past to celebrate a Main Street parade, salute veterans, pay tribute to women during World War II, and remember a historic school, to the colorful murals of Art Alley, where a crazy quilt pays homage to the Country Music Highway and Kentucky's gold mine of chart-topping country music legends.

See the first indoor shopping mall built in Kentucky at the historic Camayo Arcade. Pick up a Butter Beer and a comic book at SuperHero Creamery or blow your mad money on a flight of coveted Pappy Van Winkle at the Bourbon Bar in the downtown Delta Hotel.

Nearby, Catlettsburg's 18-hole Diamond Links Golf Course is both challenging and gorgeous, with views of surrounding hills that go on forever. In Greenup, Dragonfly Outdoor Adventures offers kayak excursions on the Little Sandy River, Grayson Lake and the Ohio River as well as cabin rentals and tent camping.

# US 23 Country Music Highway

Ashland to Pikeville • kentuckytourism.com/music/country-music-highway

☑ Loretta Lynn, the Judds, Dwight Yoakam, Larry Cordle, Tom T. Hall, Ricky Skaggs, Crystal Gayle, Patty Loveless, Billy Ray Cyrus, Keith Whitley, Hylo Brown. The hills of Eastern Kentucky are truly alive with the sound of music, thanks to a proliferation of homegrown talent.

Experience the music and the magic on a self-guided road trip along the Country Music Highway. A National Scenic Byway, it meanders through the hills and hollers of seven counties in Kentucky's Appalachian region, leading to key sites connected to some of country music's greatest artists.

Begin in Ashland, birthplace of the **Judds** and near the **Flatbush home of Billy Ray Cyrus**, heading south as the highway takes you to key country music moments, monuments, and museums, including **Loretta Lynn's homeplace at Butcher Hollow** in Van Lear and the **US 23 Country Music Highway Museum** in Staffordsville with its treasure trove of star memorabilia, stage costumes, and musical instruments.

Loretta Lynn's homeplace at Butcher Hollow (Photograph by John Michael. Courtesy of Paintsville Tourism)

Paramount Arts Center (Courtesy of Kentucky Tourism)

# Paramount Arts Center

1300 Winchester Ave. • 606-324-0007 • paramountartscenter.com

☑ At nearly 100 years old, this former motion picture palace, listed on the National Register of Historic Places, is only getting better. Designed and built in 1931 to show silent films, made exclusively by Paramount Studios, it quickly transitioned when talkies burst on scene and screen.

The 1,400-seat theater with ornate interior has been lovingly preserved and painstakingly restored with many of the theater's original fixtures and furnishings and to uncover the original richly colored murals of the lobby and main hall. Stepping through the brass entrance doors today feels much like being ushered into the theatre of the last century. Today this Art Deco gem is a premier and intimate performance venue for theater productions, headlining musicians, comedy acts, and more.

**Fun Fan Fact:** Billy Ray Cyrus filmed the music video for his chartbusting "Achy Breaky Heart" at the Paramount in January of 1992.

# Sal's Italian Eatery & Speakeasy

1624 Carter Ave. • 606-393-1312
salsspeakeasy.com

✓ When you spot the shiny black Flivver that looks like a mob getaway car, you're in the right place. Sal's lives it up with a gin joint theme, from the jalopy parked out front to the hidden entrance to the restaurant to an impressive cocktail bar crowded with dozens and dozens of bottles of giggle water.

And the food? Nothing short of the bees knees, starting with the fried ravioli, among other appetizer choices. It's hot and crisp and accompanied by a piquant marinara. The restaurant's signature roasted red pepper and gouda soup is a creamy bisque that will make you swoon. Salsiccia Cacciatore, Lasagne al Ragu, and other pasta dishes are joined by ribeye steak and bone-in pork chop entrées, among others—all served in a dimly lit dining room decorated with Prohibition signage. Of course, there is cannoli for dessert, not to mention tiramisu, gelato, and Italian lemon cake.

Sal's Italian Eatery & Speakeasy (Courtesy of Sal's Italian Eatery & Speakeasy)

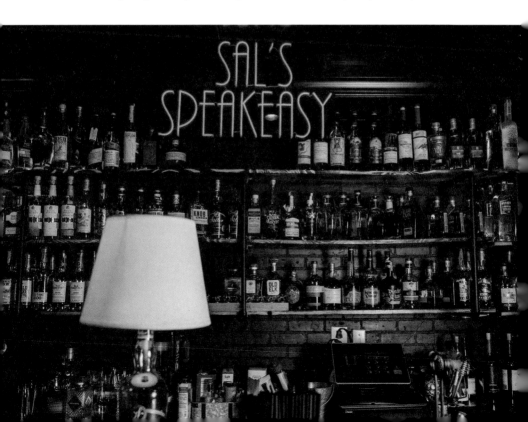

## Nearby Alternatives

### Outdoors: Port of Ashland Sculptures/Flood Wall Murals

The world's largest collection of mixed-media bronze sculptures greets visitors to this tiny river town. Venus, Vulcan, and Genesis are symbols of Ashland's beauty, culture, history, and rebirth and part of a spirited and colorful public art collection that also includes the Flood Wall Murals, each panel a significant chapter from Ashland's past.
50 15th St., 606-327-2046
visitaky.com/port-of-ashland-scluptures

### Museum: Highlands Museum & Discovery Center

Kids of all ages will find exhibits and interactive features to enjoy: composing on a Music Quilt; seeing sparkly performance costumes worn by the Judds and Loretta Lynn, among other Kentucky country music stars; crawling through a cave; climbing into a tree house; and hunting for spotted suckers in **Aqua Zone**'s giant fish tank.
1620 Winchester Ave.
606-329-8888
highlandsmuseum.com

### Outdoors: Greenbo Lake State Resort Park

Over 33 miles of trails that accommodate horses, hikers, and mountain bikers; a tranquil lake for fishing, canoeing, kayaking, and pedal boating; mini golf; a gift shop; and a swimming pool with twisty waterslide; and more—no wonder families flock to this holiday haven, home to Kentucky State Parks' only scuba refuge. Events include **Murder Mystery Dinner Theater**.
965 Lodge Rd., Greenup
606-473-7324
parks.ky.gov

### Outdoors: Carter Caves State Resort Park

Wet, muddy, exhilarating. Sumptuously forested Carter Caves is one of only two Kentucky State Parks offering subterranean adventures. Go underground on year-round tours of **Cascade Cave** and **X-Cave**. Suit up with helmet, headlamp, coveralls, and kneepads for seasonal guided tours of **Bat Cave** and **Saltpeter Cave**. Explore undeveloped **Laurel and Horn Hollow Caves** by permit.
344 Caveland Dr., Olive Hill
606-286-4411
parks.ky.gov

## Trip Planning

### Ashland Tourism and Convention Commission Board

1509 Winchester Ave.
606-329-1007, visitaky.com

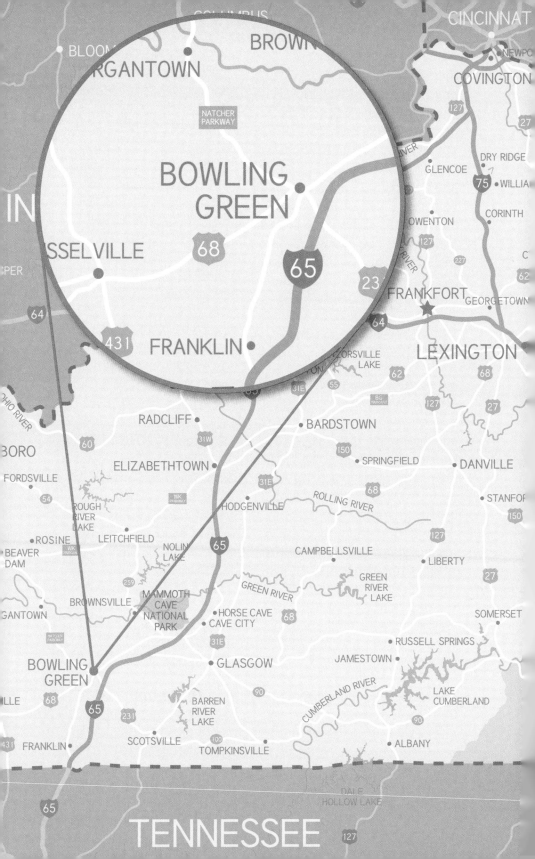

# BOWLING GREEN

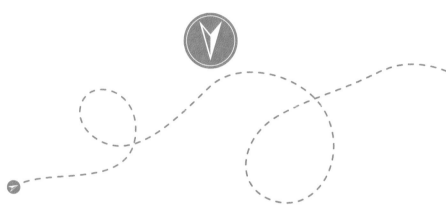

**P**LANES, TRAINS, AND AUTOMOBILES—Bowling Green is the backdrop for amazing transportation stories: America's sports car at the National Corvette Museum, the romance of the rails at the please-do-touch Historic RailPark & Train Museum, and local heroes of the sky at Aviation Heritage Park.

People stories, too: Duncan Hines, a traveling salesman turned pioneering food critic turned namesake for a brand of food products including cake mixes, gets his due at an exhibit at the free-admission Kentucky Museum, on an 80-mile scenic byway and also during June's annual Duncan Hines Days. Internationally renowned artist Joseph Dudley Downing has a museum dedicated to his fine and decorative art, which is surrounded by a lavish tapestry of Kentucky native plants within Baker Arboretum.

Create your own story, meandering along a wineries trail, stopping in at Traveler's Cellar Winery and Reid's Livery Winery. Spread a picnic packed by a local eatery in postcard-pretty Fountain Square Park. Stroll the shops tucked within yesteryear architecture to sample handmade truffles from Mary Jane's Chocolates, pour a candle at Candlemakers on the Square, or catch a free movie at the historic Capitol Arts Theatre.

# National Corvette Museum/NCM Motorsports Park/GM Corvette Assembly Plant

350 Corvette Dr. • 270-781-7973 • corvettemuseum.org

✓ For Corvette lovers, sports car fans, speed racers and wannabes, techies, and hands-on activity–loving families, Bowling Green is a bucket-list bonanza.

At the museum, follow the history of the Corvette through classic Corvette models, performance models in period vignettes, and the one-millionth Corvette made. Slide behind the wheel and race your companion in the side-by-side Corvette simulators.

Tear around the 3.2-mile racetrack in a C8 Corvette on the Corvette Experience at the NCM Motorsports Park, combining behind-the-wheel time and a learning session with track-certified instructors. Challenge the family in a high-speed go-kart race at the NCM Kartplex.

Watch a Corvette come together, piece by lustrous piece. Take the 90-minute, one-mile plant tour and witness the "marriage" of chassis and body as the parts are assembled and a brand-new Vette rolls off the assembly line to fulfill someone's dream.

National Corvette Museum (Courtesy of VisitBGKY)

Splash Lagoon (Courtesy of VisitBGKY)

# Beech Bend

798 Beech Bend Park Rd. • 270-781-7634 • beechbend.com

✓ Amusement park, water park, raceway, campground: Beech Bend is 380 acres of thrills, chills, zooms, and flumes, surrounded by stands of beech trees and spread out along the bend of the Barren River.

From family rides like bumper cars and go-karts to adrenaline-spiking roller coasters, including the award-winning Kentucky Rumbler; from the languid, lazy river at Splash Lagoon to the crazy, careening Cyclone Saucers waterslide—this park has something for everyone.

With live entertainment like Wild Bill Hiccup's Wild West Show, plus mini golf; cabana rentals; great eats at the **Tiki Grill, DJ's Diner,** and other foodie hot spots; drag racing; car shows; and more, this park doesn't know a dull moment.

Not far from the parks and raceway, Beech Bend's camping area has hundreds of wooded and waterside sites, from primitive to full hookups, for both tent and RV camping. New additions include a pair of equipped cabins next door to the bathhouse.

# Gerard's 1907 Tavern

935 College St. • 270-904-8133 • gerards1907tavern.com

☑ Settle into a warm glow of dim lighting, wood floors, and cozy brick interior and enjoy an ambience both casual and refined. Inside this turn-of-the-20th-century building adjacent to Fountain Square Park, the menu is American gourmet, the portions are hearty, and the service is friendly and flawless.

The Nashville hot chicken has the exact right amount of heat. The Weiner schnitzel is a perfect balance of tender and crisp. The house burger is topped with an intriguing mélange of smoked gouda, house coleslaw, and crispy tobacco onions topped with Henry Bain sauce, a rich, piquant steak sauce created more than a century ago by (and named after) a Louisville waiter. Each dish gets a flavor boost from locally sourced ingredients.

The bar features craft draft beer and artisanal cocktails, including an outstanding old-fashioned with a hint of smoke and seasonal martinis and cocktails. Beautifully plated desserts include a showstopper crème brûlée.

Gerard's 1907 Tavern (Courtesy of VisitBGKY)

## Nearby Alternatives

**Restaurant/Tour/Entertainment Complex: Chaney's Dairy Barn**
Santa's Cookies, Bourbon Crunch, Wow Now Brownie Cow: These are among 60 freshly made ice cream flavors at this beloved Bowling Green landmark, which also offers a lunch and dinner menu; self-guided farm tours; a playground with swings, slides, jumping pillow, and other features; and free-admission summer Moovies (bring along lawn chairs and a blanket).
**9191 Nashville Rd.**
**270-843-5567**
chaneysdairybarn.com

**Outdoors: Lost River Cave**
Hideout for train-robbing bandit Jesse James? Possibly. Home of the former Cavern Nite Club, where 1940s Big Band–era entertainers once performed? Absolutely. A boat tour of Lost River Cave is part of this family-fun urban park with hiking trails, gem mining, seasonally open **Butterfly Habitat, Nature Explore Playscape**, and gift shop.
**2818 Nashville Rd.**
**270-393-0077**
lostrivercave.org

**Outdoors: Fork in the Road**
A 21-foot-tall stainless-steel fork. A 24-foot-tall butter knife. Can a colossal spoon be far behind? Tour Franklin and Simpson County's public artscape, which also includes **Blackjack Sculpture Park**, with a spaceship alien lurking within. The "utensils" are part of the emerging 12-city Larger than Life Trail, also featuring Hopkinsville's oversized wheat sculpture. Hungry? Head to **Hot Plate**, Franklin's homestyle meat-and-three eatery.
**2018 Uhls Rd., Franklin**
**270-586-3040**
visitfranklinky.com

**Outdoors: Barren River Lake State Resort Park**
Those lazy, hazy days of summer and other seasons are the perfect time to enjoy the park's wildflower-strewn nature trails, watching the sun set from water's edge, on the end of a fishing line along the banks of the lake, or at the wheel of a golf cart gliding along an award-winning 18-hole golf course.
**1149 State Park Rd., Lucas**
**270-646-2151**
parks.ky.gov

## Trip Planning

**Bowling Green Area Convention & Visitors Bureau**
**352 Three Springs Rd.**
**800-326-7465**
visitbgky.com

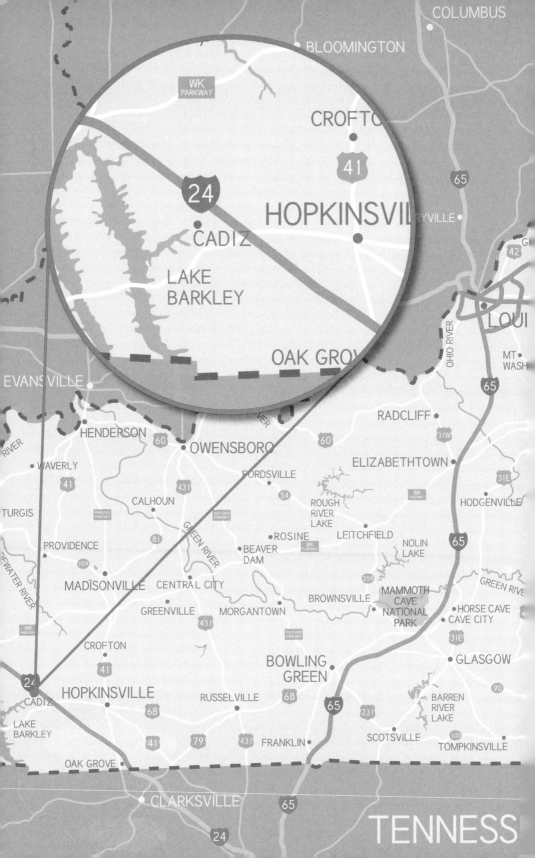

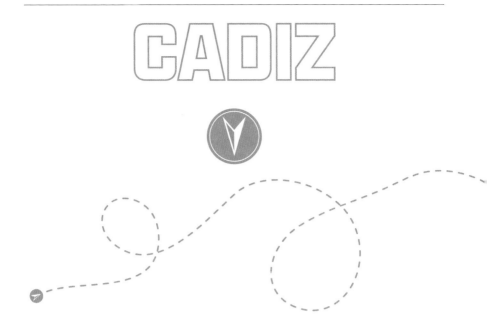

# CADIZ

**A** TINY TOWN SPILLING over with Southern charm, Cadiz is the front porch to western Kentucky's big backyard—the Land Between the Lakes National Recreation Area.

Swim, hike, kayak, and camp. Fish for catfish and crappie, dropping a line right off the banks of Lake Barkley or over the side of a boat. Jump on a giant pillow, play mini golf, or eat at a floating restaurant at the Pier at Prizer Point Marina and Resort, where you can also rent a lakeview cabin or condo as well as a pontoon with slide.

Surrounded by farmland dotted with old barns and even older cemeteries, Cadiz's Historic Downtown District is filled with restaurants dishing up down-home country cooking, antique and specialty shops, and an arts center that annually presents eight to 10 local and regional art exhibits.

In October, be bowled over by the world's largest country ham biscuit, a mammoth 400-pound delicacy baked during the Trigg County Country Ham Festival. This two-day event brings out over 200 vendors and features a carnival, food trucks, and nearly non-stop, live music from stages located at both ends of Main Street, a quilt show, and a car show—in addition to mouthwatering country ham.

# Lake Barkley State Resort Park

3500 State Park Rd. • 270-924-1131
parks.ky.gov

✓ Book a private balconied room or suite at the lodge for one of the most scenically spectacular views to be found within a state park system famous for beautiful views. The park is almost completely encircled by Lake Barkley—one of the largest man-made lakes in the eastern US, which runs parallel to nearby Land Between the Lakes National Recreation Area.

Sitting along the shoreline, the lodge overlooks the outdoor swimming pool and beyond, where pristine nature trails unwind through surrounding forests.

Showing off the lodge's soaring post-and-beam construction, the Windows on the Water Restaurant offers stunning lake views through floor-to-ceiling windows as well as Kentucky fare that can be paired with local wine and spirits.

Build sandcastles, boat, and fish. Play video games, table tennis, and 18-hole championship golf. Hike, mountain bike, and swim year-round in the heated indoor pool, part of the park's fitness center. Shop for made-in-Kentucky items in the lavishly stocked gift shop.

Lake Barkley State Resort Park (Courtesy of Kentucky State Parks)

Elk & Bison Prairie, Land Between the Lakes (Courtesy of Kentucky Tourism)

# Land Between the Lakes National Recreation Area

238 Visitor Center Dr., Golden Pond • 800-525-7077 • landbetweenthelakes.us

✔ Bordered by Kentucky Lake and Lake Barkley, this 170,000-acre forested peninsula is a playscape of wilderness, woodlands, and wildlife.

Drive the 3.5-mile paved loop for a safari experience in the Elk & Bison Prairie. Watch these majestic beasts roam and forage in a native grassland habitat that looks much like it did more than a century ago. Keep an eye out for bison calves hidden in the woods and for wallows and rubs—stumps, rocks, and trees the animals use to help them shed.

See other critters at play: butterflies, bobcats, egrets, wild turkeys, box turtles, red-tailed hawks, and songbirds. Hop a causeway of concrete "lily pads" on Hematite Lake or hike the encircling trail with wetland boardwalk to see an old-growth forest. Visit the Woodlands Nature Station or 6,800-acre Woodlands Nature Watch Area for opportunities to see hummingbirds and bald eagles.

TIP: The best elk and bison viewing opportunities are about an hour before dusk, in May and September through November.

# Harper House and Granary Piano Bar

123 D.J. Everett Dr • 270-874-2858
harperhouseky.com

✔ The silver grain bins rising in the horizon aren't for storing feed, but for serving food. Step inside this Southern steak house built inside a silo structure for a one-of-a-kind dining experience known for chef-driven cuisine.

Hickory-smoked prime rib, 12-ounce ribeye steak, and other headliners are locally sourced and highlight not only regional flavors but tastes from around the world. The atmosphere is fine dining meets rural Americana, with exposed brick walls, illuminated marquee, and live edge tables handcrafted from locally sourced and milled wood.

The restaurant has an extensive bourbon collection, a dozen rotating regional draughts, and a menu of crafted cocktails, including an award-winning signature drink, the smoky and citrusy Harper House Margarita. The bar setting is rustic, with tractor seats for barstools, horseshoes for the foot bar, and a curving bar top showing off local corn beneath an epoxy shine, a baby grand piano perched upon it. Live music is offered on weekends.

Harper House and Granary Piano Bar (Courtesy of Harper House)

## Nearby Alternatives

**Museum:** Apple Valley Hillbilly Garden and Toyland

Wacky, tacky, funky, junky—but in an irrepressibly cool roadside attraction kind of way. Curator Keith Holt has created what is surely one of the world's most original collections of nostalgia, zany fun, and full-on quirk: 3,000 yesteryear toys, outdoor "sculpture puns," a hillbilly garden, childhood memories, mannequin greeters—a tableaux of kitsch. And a story unfolds over every square inch.

**9351 US Route 68 W Calvert City, 270-366-2301**
applevalleyhillbillygardenand toyland.com

**Planetarium:** Golden Pond Planetarium and Observatory

Ahh, the night sky. Meteor showers and shooting stars, a journey through the solar system, Greek mythology's connection to the constellations—including Cetus, the sea monster—a variety of planetarium shows are offered daily in this high-resolution, fully immersive 40-foot domed theater. Laser shows, too. Summer Star Parties are held at the observatory.

**238 Visitor Center Dr., Golden Pond, 270-924-2243**
landbetweenthelakes.us

**Resort:** Patti's 1880's Settlement

Stay, play, and hide away at this all-in-one, six-acre resort village with overnight lodging and swimming pool. Dine on Southern-style deliciousness, and enjoy the tranquility garden, mini golf, gem mining, koi garden, moonshine sampling, and boutique shopping.

**1793 J H O'Bryan Ave., Grand Rivers**
**270-362-8844**
pattis1880s.com

**Museum:** Ben E. Clement Mineral Museum

Rock hounds won't be able to resist all the sparkle in this hidden gem, home to the country's largest collection of fluorite crystal specimens on display. See exquisite crystal samples of all sizes and in a spectrum of colors, as well as fossils and gemstone carvings, mining and milling artifacts, tools, photographs, and other memorabilia.

**205 N Walker St., Marion**
**270-965-4263**
clementmineralmuseum.org

## Trip Planning

Cadiz-Trigg County Tourist and Convention Commission

**5748 Hopkinsville Rd., Cadiz**
**270-522-3892**
gocadiz.com

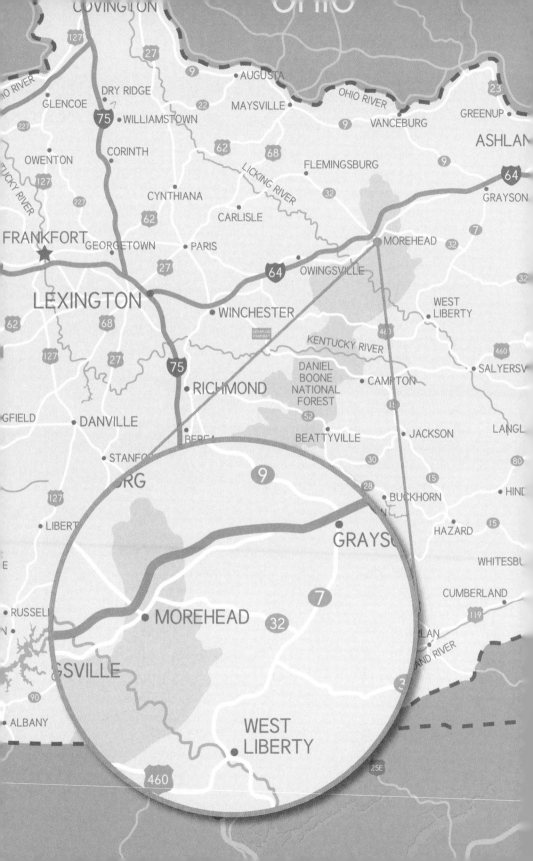

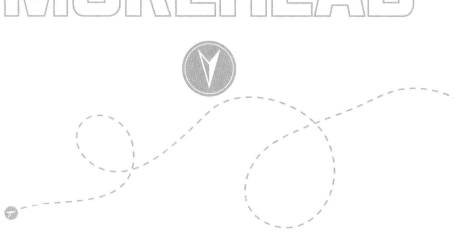

# MOREHEAD

I N THIS TOWN uniquely positioned at the trailhead of the Sheltowee Trace National Recreation Trail, visitors can grab their next read at CoffeeTree Books, share an ice cream soda at an original soda fountain at Holbrook Drug, or a classic Root Beer float served in a frosty mug from the local A&W, and hike a section of "the Trace" that spans the Daniel Boone National Forest and beyond—without ever leaving Main Street.

A picturesque college town set in the foothills of the Appalachian Mountains, Morehead knows how to enchant visitors. Catch a cosmically colorful show at Star Theater, the Space Science Center's state-of-the-art digital planetarium at Morehead State University. Read a children's storybook as it unfolds along the StoryWalk® at Rodburn Hollow Park, then spread a picnic and splash about the creek.

Besides boutiques, museums, and art galleries, Morehead is home to September's Poppy Mountain Music Festival—the largest bluegrass music festival in the country. The seasonal Maker's Market, with locally produced food and crafts and live music, sets up shop on the lawn of the Rowan County Arts Center, bustling with artists exhibits, arts workshops, and Morehead Theatre Guild productions.

# Cave Run Lake

Daniel Boone National Forest • Cumberland Ranger District
KY 801 South • 606-784-6428 • usda.gov/recarea/dbnf/recarea/?recid=39320

☑ Enjoy languid, lazy days on this strikingly beautiful lake hidden away within the Daniel Boone National Forest. An 8,000-acre lake with crystal-clear waters and 200 miles of undulating shoreline, it is a water baby's idyll, with boating, tubing, swimming, skiing, and sunning on sandy beaches in a gorgeous and unspoiled wildland.

Known as the Muskie Capital of the South for its large population of these fierce freshwater predators, Cave Run Lake is among the finest muskie lakes in the country. Connected to the lake through Cave Run Lake Tailwater is the 300-acre Minor E. Clark Fish Hatchery, one of the largest freshwater fish hatcheries in the nation and an excellent area for spotting bald eagles, osprey, raptors, and other bird species.

Two shady campgrounds, the 700-acre Twin Knobs and smaller wooded peninsula of Zilpo—each with RV and tent camping—offer a variety of amenities, including swimming beaches, boat ramps, bath houses, and stores with camping supplies.

Cave Run Lake (Courtesy of Morehead-Rowan County Tourism)

# Sheltowee Trace National Recreation Trail

Daniel Boone National Forest · Cumberland Ranger District
KY 801 South · 606-784-6428 · fs.usda.gov

✓ From its northern terminus in Morehead, this trail stretches over 300 miles to the Big South Fork National River and Recreation Area and beyond into Tennessee. Considered the "backbone" of the trail system within Daniel Boone National Forest, it is the connecting point to a network of other trails, including loops ideal for day hiking and longer, multiday trails.

The trail is named for pioneering explorer Daniel Boone, who was captured by the Shawnee Indians in winter of 1778 while traveling along Kentucky's Licking River. Boone was adopted by Chief Blackfish, who gave him the name Sheltowee, meaning "Big Turtle." The white diamond trail markers bearing the image of a turtle guide hikers along the paths.

The trail is scenic, challenging, and rugged (strenuously so in parts), wandering along narrow ridges, crossing streams, and dipping into gorges. Although the trail is open year-round, springtime especially lures hikers with wildflowers and waterfalls, and fall captivates with trees flaunting a rich palette of color.

(Courtesy of Holbrook Drug)

# Pasquale's Pizza & Pasta

182 E Main St. • 606-784-9111 • eatpasquales.com

☑ This local foodie fave may be one of the few restaurants located in a downtown listed on the National Register of Historic Places that also sits on a National Recreation Trail. But that's where hungry diners find Pasquale's—across from vintage storefronts housing Morehead originals like Sawstone Brewing and Taproom and Fuzzy Duck Coffee Shop, catty-cornered to Freedom Park on the grounds of the Rowan County Arts Center, and on the trailhead of the Sheltowee Trace.

Family owned and operated, Pasquale's has fed generations of locals and visitors alike. The restaurant is known for its cheese fries, a deliciously sloppy mess of french fries broiled with cheddar jack cheese, piled with bacon and green onion, and doused with house-made ranch dressing. Other signature dishes include strombolis, specialty pizzas, and hot sandwiches.

The restaurant has casual indoor and counter seating as well as outdoor seating. The building's exterior provides the canvas for Morehead's welcome mural.

Pasquali's (Courtesy of Morehead-Rowan County Tourism)

## Nearby Alternatives

**Museum:** Kentucky Folk Art Center at Morehead State University

Explore the color, texture, and whimsy of 1,400 creations by self-taught artists arrayed in the galleries of the historic early 1900s Union Grocery Co. building: paintings, wood carvings, textiles, and sculptural assemblages. The center presents rotating and special exhibitions, artist receptions, and an annual Appalachian Holiday Arts & Crafts Fair, and it has one of the region's finest gift shops.

102 W 1st St.
606-783-2204
facebook.com/kyfolkart

**Historic Downtown:** Mt. Sterling

Visit century-old buildings that house boutique stores and trendy restaurants in Historic Downtown Mt. Sterling in the foothills of the Appalachians. Stroll red-brick streets to see beautiful murals and vibrant public art, including Umbrella Alley. Drop by the Gateway Regional Arts Center for events, including "meet the artist," live music, and beer garden gatherings.

124 N Maysville St., Mt. Sterling
859-498-8732
mtsterlingtourism.com

**Outdoors:** Eagle Trace Golf Course

An exceptionally beautiful golf course with lush and gently rolling hills and wide, sloping fairways framed by woods, this 18-hole, par 72 course presents a variety of water, sand, and topographical challenges any golfer will appreciate. Open year-round, it has a clubhouse with Pro Shop, a concession area with seating, and a covered pavilion.

1275 Eagle Dr., 606-783-9073
eagletracegolfcourse.com

**Retro Outing:** Judy Drive-In Theater

Warm-weather weekends are made for piling into the car and catching a movie or two on the big screen at a mom-and-pop drive-in that has been showing first-run movies since 1952. Grab a spot and some funnel cakes, chili dogs with homemade sauce, and the house specialty, the Judy Burger, and settle in under the stars.

4078 Maysville Rd., Mt. Sterling
859-498-1960
judydrivein.com

## Trip Planning

Morehead Rowan County Tourism Commission

150 E 1st St.
606-780-4342
visitmorehead.com

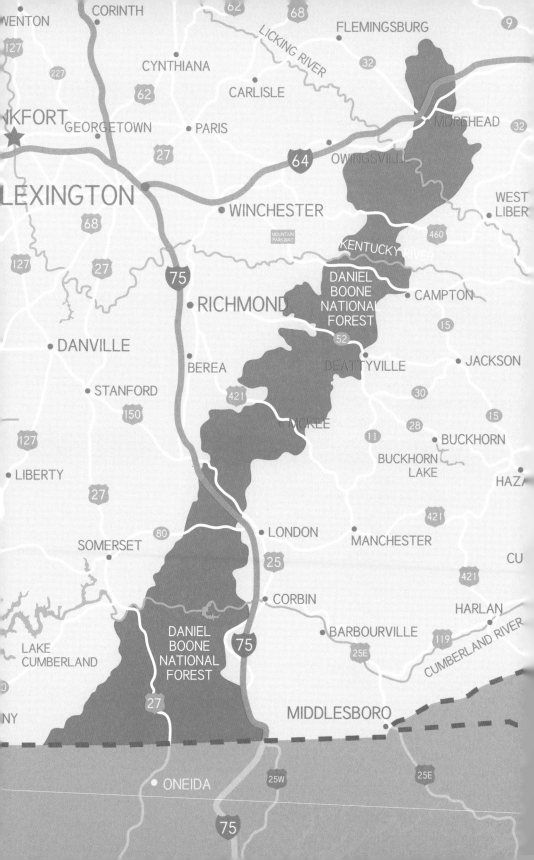

# DANIEL BOONE NATIONAL FOREST

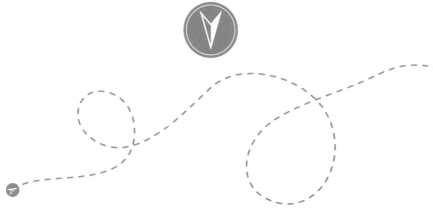

**N**AME YOUR WILDERNESS pleasure: camping, hiking, fishing, climbing, swimming, picnicking. All of these are waiting for adventurers in Daniel Boone National Forest, which spreads across 21 Kentucky counties and over more than 700,000 acres and encompasses Natural Bridge State Resort Park and Red River Gorge.

Here the landscape is defined by a rugged terrain of forested slopes, towering sandstone cliffs, narrow ravines, and sharp ridges through which more than 600 miles of trails traverse, including Sheltowee Trace National Recreation Trail.

In this vast wildland of unceasing wonder are two wilderness areas, undeveloped wildlife management areas, wetlands, and waterfalls, including Van Hook Falls with a 40-foot plummet and Flat Lick Falls, a 30-foot fall accented by lush foliage, surrounding caves, and a woodland setting.

It is home to an impressive number of natural arches—not surprising since Kentucky has more natural arches than any other state in the eastern United States. The majestic and massive stone sculptures, formed by wind and water, are a sight to behold.

# Red River Gorge Geological Area

Gladie Visitor Center • 3451 Sky Bridge Rd., Stanton
606-663-8100 • gofindoutdoors.org/sites/gladie

☑ Mother Nature gone wild, showing off her finest handiwork in this vast wilderness, a landscape raw and untamed, both dreamy and dramatic, with sandstone arches, soaring cliffs, hidden caves, waterfalls, and natural bridges.

Grab climbing harness and helmet for world-class rock climbing and scale the crags at Miller-Fork Recreational Preserve or the Motherlode in the Bald Rock Recreation Preserve. Go underground in a custom-built boat to uncover gorge history and mystery with the Gorge Underground. Rocket along five zip lines at speeds up to 55 miles per hour and 300 feet above the Red with Red River Gorge Ziplines. Tool along the scenic byway and enter the mysterious Nada Tunnel, created more than a century ago by blasting through solid sandstone.

Hike, backcountry camp, canoe, kayak, mountain bike, fish, swim, and take in some amazing and only-here wildlife viewing. Birders, take note: this National Natural Landmark is Kentucky's only known breeding site for red-breasted nuthatches.

Princess Falls at Red River Gorge Geological Area (Courtesy of Kentucky Tourism)

Natural Bridge State Resort Park (Courtesy of Kentucky State Parks)

# Natural Bridge State Resort Park
2135 Natural Bridge Rd., Slade
606-663-2214 • parks.ky.gov

✔ You may feel a bit weak in the knees crossing the 30-foot-wide "sidewalk" known as Natural Bridge. This geologic stunner—a 900-ton sandstone arch—is suspended 65 feet in the air and spans 78 feet in length, and it gifts hikers with extravagant treetop views of Red River Gorge.

To reach Natural Bridge, grab a seat on the Skylift (April through October) and ride a mile up the mountain or hike Trail #1, the original trail built in the 1890s. It winds upward through a forest of white pine, hemlock, and tulip trees (the latter of which is Kentucky's state tree) and, in the summertime, exuberant bursts of rhododendron. Either path rewards with stunning views, especially glorious during fall foliage season.

Wherever you go in the park—balconied room at **Hemlock Lodge, Sandstone Arches Restaurant** or **Trails End Tavern, Mill Creek Lake** for fishing or paddling—you'll be surrounded by lush forests and towering sandstone cliffs.

# Miguel's Pizza

1890 Natural Bridge Rd., Slade • 606-663-1975 • miguelspizza.com

☑ Don't let the unassuming exterior fool you—this pizza place, located in a historic former 1940s store across the street from **Natural Bridge State Resort Park**, serves pies that pack a (delicious) punch, with multiple sauce and cheese choices and up to 40 different toppings, including kielbasa, tofu, and mango salsa. And no one goes to **Red River Gorge** without making a stop here.

Breakfast, lunch, and dinner; cold beer and hot spiced cider, slushie margaritas, and Kentucky's own Ale-8-One soft drink; basketball and sand volleyball courts; lots of outdoor seating and a laid-back, everybody's-friends kind of vibe—if you're hiking the Red, Miguel's should be on the agenda.

It is a one-stop shop with gear for outdoor adventurers at the adjacent Miguel's Rock Climbing Shop and a variety of accommodations—from a two-bedroom cabin to the castle-like lodge house with nine bedrooms, to a three-apartment unit—through **Red River Gorge Retreats**.

Miguel's Pizza (Courtesy of Kentucky Tourism)

## Nearby Alternatives

### Culinary Trail: Beer Cheese Trail

Cheese zealots: rejoice! Savor an original Kentucky delicacy, beer cheese, where it all began: Winchester, birthplace of beer cheese. Download the Beer Cheese Digital Passport and taste your way to 15 stops—each offering a unique flavor spin with a signature beer cheese dish. Beer cheese highball, anyone? The **Beer Cheese Festival** takes place every June.

**61 S Main St., Winchester**
**859-744-0556**
visitwinchesterky.com

### Music Venue/Museum: Renfro Valley Entertainment Center

Known for its rich history of country music, Kentucky's Country Music Capital is an entertainment complex that includes the storied Old Barn Theatre, New Barn Theatre, shopping village, and RV park. Next door, the **Kentucky Music Hall of Fame & Museum** celebrates music of all genres through interactive displays, artists' performance costumes, live music events, and more.

**2380 Richmond St., Mt. Vernon**
**800-514-3849**
renfrovalley.com

**606-256-1000**
kentuckymusichalloffame.com

### Accommodations: Red River Gorgeous

From couples-only and family-friendly twin tree houses with slide and hot tub to geodesic domes suspended in the treetops to an extreme cliff dweller bolted to a sandstone cliff line—think Swiss Family Robinson given the full glamping upgrade—these canopy hideaways have heat, A/C, gas stove, French press coffee pot—and views to die for.

**3546 Nada Tunnel Rd., Stanton**
**606-663-9824**
rrgcabin.com

### Music Venue: The Barnyard Entertainment Venue

Countryside concerts and comedy shows; a summer filled with country, rock, Christian, and bluegrass music performances; nights set aside for family fun and fireworks: quality live entertainment unfolds beneath the stars at this open-air amphitheater surrounded by 170 rolling acres. Tents and RVs are welcome at the primitive campground.

**10005 W Hwy. 36, Sharpsburg**
**606-709-2276**
thebarnyardvenue.com

## Trip Planning

### Daniel Boone National Forest

fs.usda.gov/dbnf

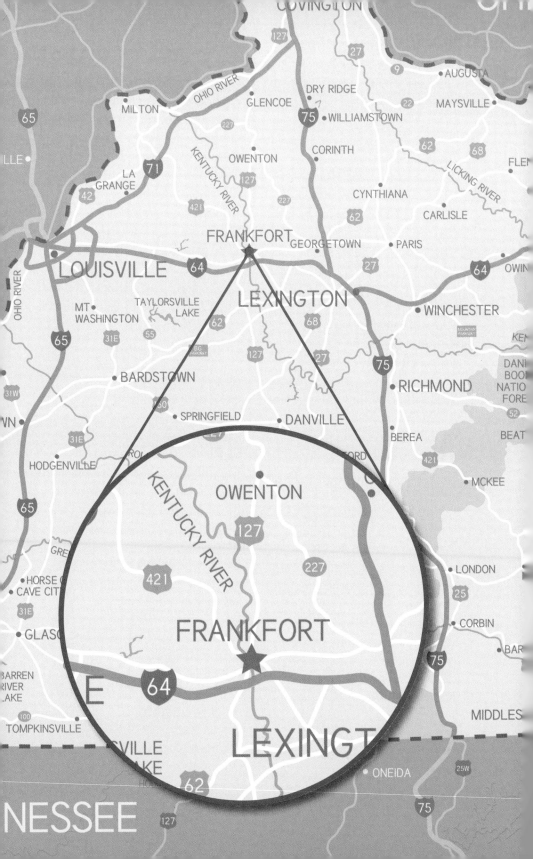

# FRANKFORT

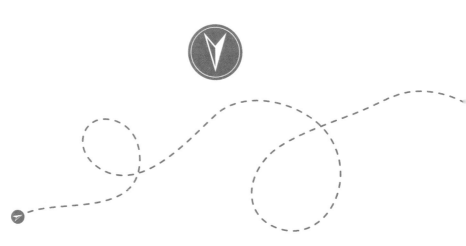

**H**ISTORIC, ARTISTIC, AND architecturally beautiful with its mix of Greek Revival, Gothic Revival, Georgian, and Italian Renaissance–style buildings, Kentucky's capital city brings the panache of world-class bourbon distilleries, including Buffalo Trace and Castle & Key, and a sophisticated arts landscape of evocative and provocative sculptures and murals into a small-town setting.

Ride the free (seasonal) Frankfort Trolley for a narrated tour that includes the Kentucky State Capitol, considered one of the most impressive capitols in the country, its stunning opulence accented with tulip gardens, massive Floral Clock, and the little-known treasure of the First Ladies Miniature Doll Collection.

Catch a classic movie in the Grand Theatre, a 1911 vaudeville house that once showed silent movies. Pop into Capital City Museum to see exquisitely handmade bait-casting reels among the exhibits. Throw a pot at Broadway Clay.

Stop by Frankfort Cemetery and pay respects to frontier explorer Daniel Boone. Take an easy hike to the waterfalls at Cove Spring Park. Say hello to a 670-pound black bear at Salato Wildlife Education Center, a small zoo inhabited by 300 animals native to Kentucky.

# Buffalo Trace Distillery®

113 Great Buffalo Trace • 502-783-1000 • buffalotracedistillery.com

✓ Tour the grounds where the "Father of the Modern Bourbon Industry," Colonel Edmund Haynes (E. H.) Taylor Jr. once distilled spirits. See the one-story stone **Old Taylor House**, built in 1792 and still standing at this National Historic Landmark. The family-owned, legendary spirit maker Buffalo Trace has a tradition of fine bourbon dating back over 200 years, one that survived the Great Fire of 1882, the Prohibition years of the early 20th century, the Great Flood of 1937, and other calamities.

Reserve a complimentary tour, which includes tasting award-winning spirits, and learn how this distillery was one of a mere handful to receive a permit to bottle "medicinal" whiskey during the failed "Noble Experiment." Step into an archaeological dig site at **OFC Distillery**—the very one E. H. purchased and named for producing fine whiskey in old-fashioned wood-fired copper stills—called "Bourbon Pompeii." Experience the history, innovation, and thoughtful experimentation of the oldest continuously operating distillery in America.

Buffalo Trace Distillery® (Courtesy of Frankfort Tourist Commission)

Kentucky River Tours' Bourbon Boat (Courtesy of Frankfort Tourist Commission)

# Kentucky River Tours' Bourbon Boat

701 Wilkinson Blvd. • 502-219-3318
kyrivertours.com

Channel your inner Indiana Jones for the wildly popular Old Taylor Tour, combining Kentucky River lore with a visit to **Buffalo Trace Distillery**'s "Bourbon Pompeii" and a chance to follow in the footsteps of E. H. Taylor Jr. Or join a Stave & Thief–certified bourbon concierge for a cruise on the Kentucky River combined with an onboard barrel pick tasting.

The "Bourbon Boat," the only boat-based bourbon tour in the country, offers a variety of themed river tours focusing on the important role the river has played in the making of Kentucky's signature drink.

Board the 14-passenger *Trace of Kentucky* or the larger *Bourbon Belle* for a cruise into bourbon history, passing bourbon distilleries lost to time and temperance along the way. Learn about Kentucky's capital city and the bourbon industry on the Kentucky River Historical Frankfort Tour. Book the Kentucky River Historical Lock Through and pass through the circa-1840s Lock and Dam #4.

# Serafini

243 W Broadway St. • 502-875-5599 • serafinifrankfort.com

☑ This casual fine-dining bistro overlooking the Greek Revival–style circa-1793 Old State Capitol is a favorite lunchtime haunt of local politicians. Charmingly set in a corner location in the heart of downtown Frankfort, the restaurant pairs Italian and Kentucky fusion fare with a curated menu of bourbon, wine, beer, and classic cocktails that shows off some of Kentucky's finer spirits: the Boulevardier (made with Buffalo Trace bourbon), a Bourbon Sidecar featuring Bulleit Bourbon, and an old-fashioned poured with Woodford Reserve, among others.

Serafini's checks a lot of boxes for a memorable meal: the chef's commitment to using local ingredients, a historical setting and unhurried and relaxing ambience, live jazz on select evenings, outdoor seating on a brick-paved sidewalk, friendly waitstaff, and bartenders who not only mix a superb cocktail but also spin stories about their provenance and share tips for area sightseeing.

Serafini (Courtesy of Frankfort Tourist Commission)

## Nearby Alternatives

**Museum: Thomas D. Clark Center for Kentucky History**

Take a "Kentucky Journey" guided by museum staff through 12,000 years and 3,000 items. This Smithsonian Affiliate, headquarters of the Kentucky Historical Society, is the steward of artifacts encompassing the profound (like Abraham Lincoln's personal pocket watch) to the prosaic (the handmade quilts, tools, and furniture that tell the story of everyday Kentuckians).

**100 W Broadway St.**
**502-564-1792**
history.ky.gov/visit/thomas-d-clark-center-for-kentucky-history

**Outdoors: Josephine Sculpture Park**

Please do touch the art at Kentucky's only sculpture park. Climb on it, too. Explore 70 contemporary sculptures created by artists from around the world and planted throughout the 30-acre native meadow and forested areas of this free-admission outdoor gallery. Enjoy art, concerts, workshops—and a chance to add your own artistic flourish to the *GRAPHOLOGYHENGE* exhibit.

**3355 Lawrenceburg Rd.**
**502-352-7082**
josephinesculpturepark.org

**Factory Tour: Rebecca Ruth Candy Tours & Museum**

Meet the "Mother of Bourbon Balls" on a candy and museum tour. Sample an original secret-recipe bourbon ball—invented by Ruth Hanly Booe in 1938—a sweet treat featuring a creamy bourbon center with a kick, dipped in Rebecca Ruth's dark chocolate, and crowned with a pecan. The fourth generation of Booes continue the handcrafted chocolate-making traditions.

**116 E 2nd St.**
**502-223-7475**
rebeccaruthonline.com

**Outdoors/Brewery: West Sixth Farm**

Taproom, trails, and tacos. A hopyard, cider apple orchard, food truck, picnic grounds, and catch-and-release fishing pond surround West Sixth Brewery's taproom. Multiuse nature trails for walkers, runners, hikers, and mountain bikers dart off into the back forty of this 120-acre farm. Hours vary by season.

**4495 Shadrick Ferry Rd.**
**859-705-0915**
westsixth.com/farm

## Trip Planning

**Frankfort Tourist Commission**
300 Saint Clair St., Ste. 102
502-875-8687, visitfrankfort.com

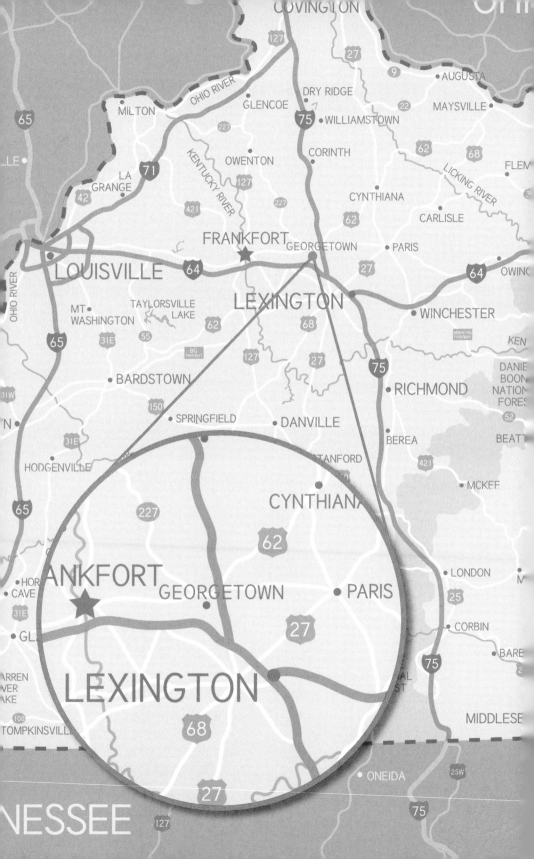

# GEORGETOWN

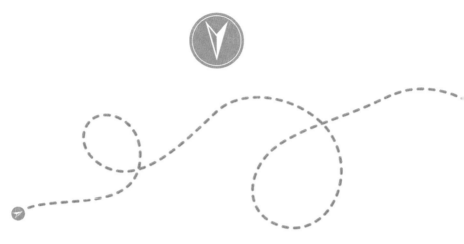

**T**HE STORY OF Georgetown, Kentucky's Horse Headquarters and Birthplace of Bourbon, is inextricably intertwined with one of the most prominent movers and shakers of the bourbon world. For it is here, on the banks of Royal Spring on the edge of downtown Georgetown, where the story of bourbon began in 1789, with Baptist minister Rev. Elijah Craig and his auspicious discovery of the bourbon distillation process.

Not only is Craig considered the Father of Bourbon, but he is also the founder of Georgetown, a forward-thinking community that meticulously preserves its past. Georgetown's pristine, Victorianesque Downtown Historic District is a shopper's and foodie's delight, home to dozens of independently owned shops, boutiques, art galleries, and restaurants.

When Craig arrived in the area in 1786, he brought with him a spirit of innovation and entrepreneurialism that can be seen today in such technologically empowered enterprises as Toyota Motor Manufacturing Kentucky—the world's largest Toyota manufacturing plant and home of the Toyota Camry, RAV4 Hybrid, and Lexus ES350—and the state-of-the-art Blue Run Spirits distillery, expected to open in 2025.

Georgetown is home to award-winning Country Boy Brewing; the gracious Ward Hall, one of the great architectural masterpieces of America; and several Kentucky Proud family-fun farms.

# Toyota Kentucky Experience Center

1001 Cherry Blossom Way · 502-570-6572
tourtoyota.com/kentucky

✔ Toyota Motor Manufacturing Kentucky offers a unique opportunity to go behind the scenes at the company's oldest and largest facility in North America. Take a free-admission tour of the Experience Center to see one of the most fully integrated manufacturing plants anywhere in the world—complete with on-site plastics, power train, and die manufacturing facilities.

Watch the center's 20-foot interactive 3D projected map come to life to give an immersive look at the work that takes place every day across Toyota's 1,300-acre campus. A manufacturing wall gives a sneak peek at some of the unique processes in the manufacturing system. Another exhibit shines a light on the company's commitment to the local community.

A product kiosk explains the research and engineering that go into each of the vehicles Toyota builds at this facility; training demos teach the same fundamental skills Toyota team members practice and master; and a power train display showcases the various engine types built here.

**TIP:** Don headphones and safety glasses for the free tram tour through the plant, a fascinating integration of precision, people, skill, automation, and robotics.

Toyota Kentucky Experience Center (Courtesy of Toyota North America)

Old Friends Thoroughbred Retirement Farm (Courtesy of Kathryn Witt)

# Old Friends Thoroughbred Retirement Farm

1841 Paynes Depot Rd. • 502-863-1775 • oldfriendsequine.org

Visitors to this aftercare facility for retired Thoroughbreds find a whole herd of celebrities. In fact, 175 four-legged luminaries spend their golden years here, living their best life on the rolling green pastureland, including 1997 Kentucky Derby and Preakness winner Silver Charm, a 2007 inductee into the Racing Hall of Fame; 2002 Belmont Stakes winner, Sarava; and 2011 Belmont Stakes winner Ruler on Ice.

These champs and others are always up for carrots, cuddles, selfies, and photo ops—and a chance to relive their glory days. Meet 15 or so of the residents on guided tours, including a special tour with Michael Blowen, the former *Boston Globe* film critic who founded Old Friends in 2003.

You might also encounter Little Silver Charm, a miniature horse named after his idol, the aforementioned (big) Silver Charm, and coauthor of *A Charmed Life*, which chronicles the story of Old Friends and its mission.

# Fava's

159 E Main St. • 502-863-4383 • facebook.com/favasofgeorgetown

☑ You don't argue with a diner that has been around since 1910. You simply dig into the vittles: signature breakfasts like the Country Boy with eggs, country ham, pork tenderloin, hash browns, biscuit, and creamy sausage gravy; and hearty lunches like fried catfish, thick-cut bologna, pimento cheese sandwiches, Fava's crispy, seasoned chips, and more. This is grandma-approved cookin'.

Located in the heart of downtown Georgetown, Fava's is so beloved a restaurant and such a fixture on the local dining landscape that author Nick Allen Brown featured it in his gripping novel *Field of Dead Horses*. The book is set in Georgetown and tells the story of an 80-year-old small-town secret.

It may or may not mention Fava's decadent homemade pies—butterscotch, chocolate, coconut, and lemon cream heaped with meringue, and apple, cherry, pumpkin, and pecan fruit pies. See what's in the case, then order, eat, smile, repeat. It's that good.

Fava's (Courtesy of Georgetown/Scott County Tourism)

## Nearby Alternatives

**Outdoors: Paris Horse Farm Tours**

Two iconic farms. Two unforgettable experiences. At Claiborne, tour the legendary farm—from traditional breeding shed to cemetery—that has produced dozens of champions, including 1973 Triple Crown winner Secretariat. Meet Thoroughbreds' matriarchs (mothers, grandmothers, and great-grandmothers of champs) at Our Mims Retirement Haven, where "the Ladies" spend their golden years.

**703 Winchester Rd., Paris 859-987-2330,**
claibornefarm.com
**2810 Millersburg Ruddles Mill Rd., Paris, 859-312-9979**
ourmims.org

**French Connection: Downtown Paris**

Paris shows its *joie de vivre* with its very own smaller-scale replica Eiffel Tower illuminated at night; the world's largest mural of Thoroughbred racing champ Secretariat; the world's tallest three-story building (with penthouse suite accommodations); and Kentucky cooking at Trackside Restaurant and Bourbon Bar at the historic Paris Train Depot.

**Paris-Bourbon County Tourism Commission, 806 Main St. Paris, 859-987-8744**
pariskytourism.com

**Gardens: Yuko-en on the Elkhorn**

Step through the garden's Tokugawa Gates and enter a world of color, fragrance, graceful sculptural elements, and serenity. Pack a blanket, pick up a picnic from a Georgetown restaurant, and head to the Kentucky-Japan Friendship Garden. The four-season, five-acre Japanese-style strolling garden is like a spa visit for the senses and the soul.
**700 US-25 N, 502-603-9454**
yukoen.com

**Outdoors: Wendt's Wildlife Adventure**

Sloths, zebras, camels, kangaroos, reptiles, African porcupines, and capybara . . . see 35 different species of animals from around the world at this kid-friendly (seasonal) farm. Feed the birds at the parakeet encounter. Cool down with an ice cream or slushie at the splash pad. Explore Bushy Creek and tour the historic Daniel Boone Cabin.
**3740 Maysville Rd., Carlisle 859-405-8065**
wendtswildlife.com

## Trip Planning

**Georgetown/Scott County Tourism Office & Visitor Center**
**399 Outlet Center Dr. 502-863-2547**
georgetownky.com

CINCINNATI
NEWPORT
COVINGTON
HILLSBORO
HAZARD
WHITESBURG
421
HESTER
CUMBERLAND
421
119
HARLAN
CUMBERLAND RIVER
RVILLE
119
GLENCOE
OWENTON
GREENUP
ASHLAND
GRAYSON
FRANKFORT
LEXINGTON
WEST LIBERTY
KENTUCKY RIVER
DANIEL BOONE NATIONAL FOREST
CAMPTON
SALYERSVILLE
RICHMOND
DANVILLE
BEREA
BEATTYVILLE
JACKSON
LANGLEY
STANFORD
MCKEE
BUCKHORN
BUCKHORN LAKE
HINDMAN
LIBERTY
HAZARD
WHITESBURG
LONDON
MANCHESTER
SOMERSET
CUMBERLAND
RUSSELL SPRINGS
CORBIN
HARLAN
BARBOURVILLE
CUMBERLAND RIVER
LAKE CUMBERLAND
DANIEL BOONE NATIONAL FOREST
MIDDLESBORO
ALBANY
ONEIDA

# HARLAN & HARLAN COUNTY

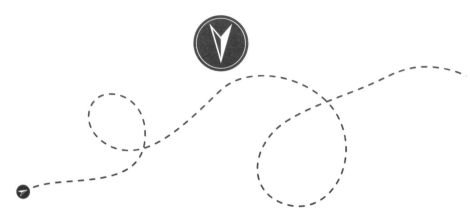

**O**NCE HOME TO the largest coal mining town in the country in Lynch, Harlan County never forgets its roots. Evidence of its coal mining past may be seen in restaurants, downtown monuments, shops like Moonbow Tipple Coffee & Sweets—even extreme adventures that take place on old strip-mining roads.

Harlan is home to Kentucky's highest peak—Black Mountain, rising 500 feet taller than any other mountain in the state—and to the Kentucky Coal Museum in Benham, a former coal camp, steward of the country's most comprehensive collection of mining memorabilia. Pine Mountain Settlement School offers visitors a chance to learn traditional folk crafts such as weaving, foraging, and identifying indigenous flora and fauna.

Downtown Harlan stays lively with a dozen boutiques, an antique and unique-finds store, a video game lounge, and the Harlan County Beer Company—the county's first (legal) brewery, offering indoor and outdoor seating and kids meals served on souvenir Frisbees. Downtown, the *Petunia the Opossum* mural shares the story of poke sallet (wild greens), and the Poke Sallet Festival—Harlan's biggest annual event—takes place in June.

# Black Mountain Off Road Park/Black Mountain Thunder Zipline

711 Bailey Creek Rd., Evarts • 606-837-3205 • blackmountainoffroad.com

☑ Prepare to get dirty—even muddy—as you face down rocky, rutted trails on Black Mountain's 150 miles of rugged terrain. Forged from old strip-mining and logging roads, the trails—rated 1 through 5 and ranging from easy to moderate to extreme—zigzag across 8,000 acres of mountain at elevations of up to 3,300 feet.

Bring your off-road vehicle, helmet, and sense of adventure to Kentucky's highest peak for a variety of off-road experiences. Although some of the trails are designated for ATVs and dirt bikes only, most are multiuse and open to all types of vehicles.

Black Mountain is also the site of Kentucky's highest, fastest, and longest zip lines: 11 lines hurl zippers along for a two-hour, two-mile canopy tour that shoots up to 500 feet high and races along at speeds of up to 60 miles an hour. When you catch your breath, you'll catch sight of the breathtaking beauty of the surrounding Appalachian Mountains.

Black Mountain Off Road Park (Courtesy of Harlan Tourism)

Blanton Forest on Pine Mountain (Courtesy of Kentucky Tourism)

# Blanton Forest State Nature Preserve

KY 840, Harlan County • 606-573-4495
harlancountytrails.com/blanton-forest

✓ What did the land that became Kentucky look like when Daniel Boone and the settlers traversed westward through the **Cumberland Gap** and into nature untamed? Enter this ancient forest on **Pine Mountain**—the largest old-growth forest in the state and one of 13 old-growth tracts remaining in the eastern US—and trace those long-erased footfalls of the first pioneers who saw these same exact trees.

Towering 100 feet into the sky and with trunks three to four feet in diameter, these trees stand as silent sentinels over mountaintop wetlands, a forest of tulip poplar, beech, hemlock, magnolia, and other tree species, with some dating back to the late 1600s. It is a haven for hikers, birders, and photographers, with some of the most incredible views to be found on **Knobby Rock Trail**.

Camp Blanton sits at the access point to Blanton Forest and offers overnight stays from rustic to more upgraded experiences in cabins with kitchens and fireplaces.

# The Portal Pizzeria

101 N Main St. • 606-573-0505 • theportalpizzeria.com

☑ More than a century ago this was a coal camp community. Today, Harlan is *Justified* country. That's right. The FX Network's long-running hit TV show is set in and around Harlan County.

While not filmed on location here, the show featured this Harlan restaurant as part of a *Justified* story arc in Season 6. Episode 2, titled "Cash Game," involved a bank heist—and considering the restaurant is tucked in the former bank, it was the perfect setting. For *Justified* fans visiting Harlan, dining at the Portal is an absolute must.

Voted the best restaurant in Harlan, the Portal is famous for hand-tossed, wood-fired pizzas, featuring scratch-made dough and sauce and dressed with gourmet toppings, including homegrown tomatoes, basil, and vegetables. It is also known for lasagna and steaks, not to mention a delectable coal nuggets dessert, deep-fried morsels of dough wrapped in chocolate and caramel, which pays tribute to Harlan history.

The Portal Pizzeria (Courtesy of the Portal Pizzeria)

## Nearby Alternatives

### Museum: Portal 31 Mine Tour/ The Kentucky Coal Museum

Go underground to Kentucky's first exhibition coal mine, which dates to 1917, and the world's largest coal camp. Pair Portal 31's kid-friendly underground railcar tour with a visit to Black Mountain for a unique experience that takes visitors from Kentucky's highest peak to deep inside the earth within a span of mere minutes.

Lynch (Harlan County)
606-848-3131
portal31.org

### Outdoors: Kingdom Come State Park

Prepare to have your breath stolen at Kentucky's highest-elevated state park from one or all of its eight accessible overlooks. Perched on the crest of Pine Mountain, this unspoiled wilderness has hiking trails, a mountain lake for fishing, and lots of planned activities, including artist-led paint classes and themed mini golf. Disco or haunted golf, anyone?

502 Park Rd., Cumberland
606-589-4138, parks.ky.gov

### Outdoors: Cumberland Gap National Historical Park

Camp where Daniel Boone, bison, Native Americans, and pioneers once slept, in the nearly impenetrable hinterlands that became the first Gateway to the West. Guided tours of **Gap Cave**, miles of trails, Civil War fortifications, ruins, wildlife, and children's programming— it's all here, along with the chance to stand in three states at once: Kentucky, Tennessee, and Virginia.

91 Bartlett Park Rd.
Middlesboro, 606-248-2817
nps.gov/cuga

### Outdoors: Pine Mountain State Resort Park

Springtime blooms of pink mountain laurel and red buds; fall foliage in shades of gold and russet. One of Kentucky's original four state parks, Pine Mountain charms with stone-trimmed lodge, concerts, festivals, Kentucky fare, impressive 25-foot **Honeymoon Falls**, and **Chained Rock** (named for the boulder perched high above Pineville). Ah, and those panoramic mountaintop views.

1050 State Park Rd., Pineville
606-337-3066
parks.ky.gov

## Trip Planning

Harlan Tourist & Convention Commission
201 S Main St., Harlan
606-573-4495
harlancountytrails.com

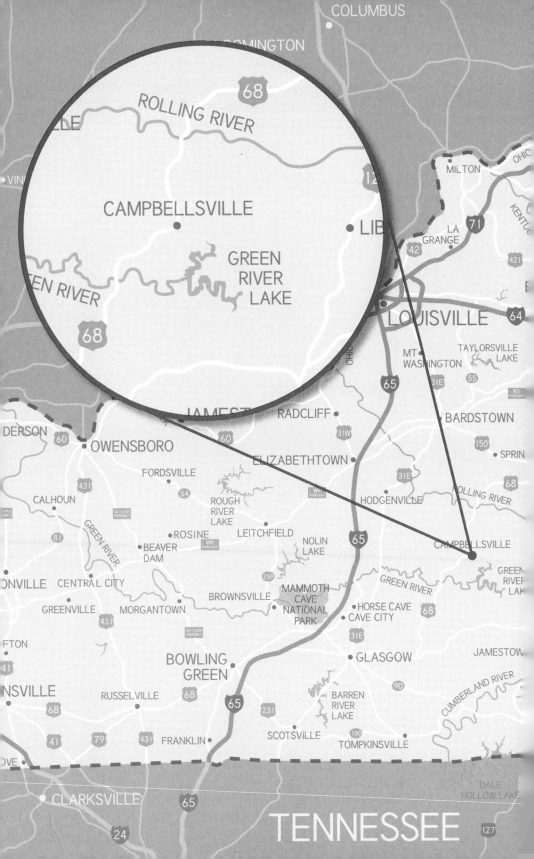

# CAMPBELLSVILLE

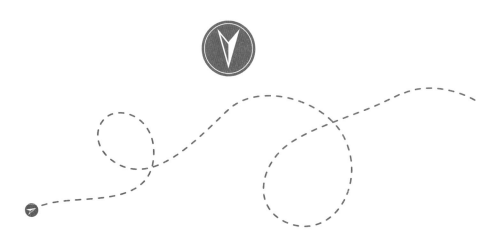

**O**NCE UPON A TIME, Campbellsville served as a stagecoach stop on the National Mail Route of the 1830s. Through decades of change and development it has retained its storybook good looks, with beautiful Italianate and Gothic Revival–style architecture lining its historic downtown district. Inviting storefronts open to independently owned businesses— clothing boutiques, home accessories shops, a bookstore, restaurants, bars, and a bakery.

Campbellsville University brings performing and fine arts to town, with a full season of shows at the Russ Mobley Theater and a collection of original jewelry, sculpture, paintings, and other artworks made by faculty, students, and staff of the college. These are arrayed inside rustic log houses comprising the Chowning Art Shop.

As a Kentucky Trail Town, Campbellsville is the front door to adventure—Green River, Green River Lake State Park, Tebbs Bend-Green River Bridge Battlefield, Trace-Pitman Greenway, the nature trails at Homeplace on Green River—while providing the comforts and convenience of shops, restaurants, entertainment, and lodging. This being Kentucky, that means a Bourbon Boutique as well, a combination bar/lounge/game space/live music venue.

# Quiet Woods Green River Stables

592 Robin Rd. • 270-789-4525
greenriverstables.com

☑ Saddle up your horse at this cowpoke's dream getaway and lope along the shoreline of Green River Lake and into miles of wooded trails within heavily forested Green River Lake State Park, spotting wild turkey, foxes, and other wildlife along the way.

At the end of the day, stop by the saloon for refreshments, a little karaoke, or live musical entertainment, or relax around the firepit at your campsite, roasting marshmallows and watching for shooting stars in the open skies above.

A 17-acre hideaway located less than two miles from the state park, the Quiet Woods horse and RV campground has 93 full-hookup sites, bathhouses, and laundry rooms. Star House, a three-bedroom cottage with a comfortable farmhouse feel, full kitchen, and a front porch overlooking the surrounding woods, is tucked at the back of the campground. And don't worry about your ride; horses are accommodated in the nearby covered 50-stall stable.

Quiet Woods Green River Stables (Courtesy of Taylor County Tourist Commission)

Great River Lake State Park (Courtesy of Kentucky State Parks)

# Green River Lake State Park

179 Park Office Rd. • 270-465-8255
parks.ky.gov/explore/green-river-lake-state-park-7814

☑ With uninterrupted miles of shoreline, Green River Lake is the jewel of Green River, a family-friendly lake surrounded by 23,000 acres of forested land with beautiful, natural views and a homey atmosphere.

Pitch a tent or park the RV right along the shoreline (the entire campground is located on the lake). Wake up to the sun rising over the water and revel in a day of rest, relaxation, and recreation: boating, skiing, kayaking, swimming, sunning on the beach, and fishing for catfish, bluegill, bass, and crappie; hiking, biking, and horseback riding on nearly 30 miles of multipurpose trails; playing basketball, volleyball, and 18-hole miniature golf; picnicking at shady spots and swinging, sliding, and climbing at the playground.

Share pizza or cool off with ice cream at the marina. Shop for souvenirs at the **Green River Gift Shop**. Take a walk or drive to see eagles, deer, and other wildlife. In the fall, enjoy the show of color sweeping through the trees.

**TIP:** Kentucky State Parks has nine parks with swimming beaches and Green River Lake State Park is one of them.

# Druther's Restaurant

101 N Columbia Ave. • 270-465-3870 • druthersrestaurant.com

✓ This restaurant chain began life in 1956 as Burger Queen and eventually rebranded in 1981 to Druther's—but even its snappy jingle, "I'd Ruther Go to Druther's Restaurant," couldn't keep the franchise from eventually slipping into restaurant history.

Except for one.

The Campbellsville location of Druther's—the last independent Druther's in the world—recalls the glory days of this eatery known for juicy burgers and perfectly seasoned, crunchy fried chicken. Both menu items are still served today, and with a generous side of nostalgia—not to mention golden, fresh, and flaky buttery biscuits that accompany a hearty Druther's breakfast served any time of day.

The restaurant's recipe for success dates to 1970: It is family owned and operated, warm, clean, and inviting, and it sticks to what it does best—preparing Southern comfort-food classics served in a casual setting.

Druther's Restaurant (Courtesy of Taylor County Tourist Commission)

## Nearby Alternatives

### Retro Outing: Skyline Drive-In

"Let's all go to the lobby to get ourselves a treat." Roll back the clock to the 1950s and 1960s as you pull in beneath the stars and the giant outdoor screen for an old-school family movie night. It's cash only at the gate (cash and card at the concessions) for first-run flicks—two shown each weekend night beginning at dusk.

**5600 Hodgenville Rd. Summersville, 270-973-5005**
skylinedrivein.com

### Outdoors: Green River Paddle Trail

This trail is the prime spot to start or finish a kayak adventure on Green River. It begins at the spillway below the Green River Lake Dam, includes parts of Little Barren River and Russell Creek, and offers a slew of activities including canoeing, fishing, and wildlife watching. Cabins and RV hookups are available, too.

**205 W Columbia Ave. Greensburg, 270-789-2956**
facebook.com/greenriverpaddletrips

### Outdoors: Taylor County Quilt Trail

Wild Goose Chase, Tobacco Leaf, Diamonds Are Forever. All are among a baker's dozen of quilt squares seen on this barn quilt driving tour that shows off Kentucky's quilt-making heritage as well as farmland, scenic back roads, and natural beauty. The trail edges along part of **Green River Lake State Park** before dipping further into the county.

**270-465-3786**
kentuckytourism.com/explore/scenic-barn-quilt-driving-tour-3482

### Small-Town Fun: Liberty

See an exact replica of the original Liberty Bell in this cute-as-a-bug's-ear town, home of the **Casey County Apple Festival** (September), featuring the World's Largest Apple Pie. Shop downtown boutiques and Amish and Mennonite shops in the surrounding countryside. Kayak or fish Lake Liberty. Enjoy wildflowers and lake views on the **Lake Liberty nature trail**.

**Liberty Tourism & Convention Commission**
**518 Middleburg St., Liberty**
**606-706-7777**
explorelibertyky.com

## Trip Planning

**Taylor County Tourist Commission**
**325 E Main St.**
**270-465-3786**
campbellsvilleky.com

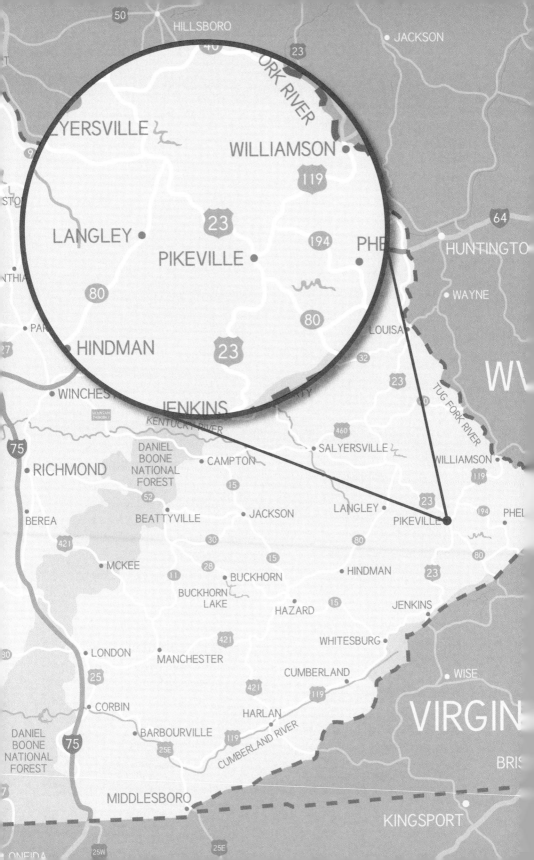

# PIKEVILLE

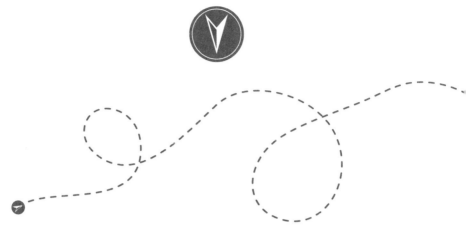

**A** MOM-AND-POP MAIN STREET set against a verdant mountain backdrop. An engineering marvel that sets the stage for magnificent views. Pikeville, "the city that moves mountains," is famous for being the site of the infamous Hatfield and McCoy Feud that started with a hog, spanned two centuries, and left a trail of dead bodies in its wake.

Visitors from around the world find their way to eastern Kentucky for this authentic experience. Another one? Standing atop the Pikeville Cut-through and being blown away by views of surrounding mountains and the valley far, far below.

Be charmed by a Bear Affair and its sleuth of bears—Hatfield and McCoy, Hillbilly and Moonshine bears, among others—striking a pose in Pikeville's historic downtown district. Part of the town's public arts scene, the bears honor the University of Pikeville's sports mascot.

Shop independently owned stores. Dine in locally owned restaurants. Sample moonshine at Dueling Barrels Distillery and Brewery. And catch homegrown theater with big-name, family-fun entertainment at the Appalachian Center for the Arts.

# Hatfields & McCoys Historic Feud Sites/Driving Tour

Pikeville-Pike County Visitors Center • 831 Hambley Blvd.
606-432-5063 • tourpikecounty.com

☑ "Two households, both alike in dignity/In fair Verona, where we lay our scene/From ancient grudge break to new mutiny/ Where civil blood makes civil hands unclean." Substitute the Hatfields and McCoys for the Montagues and Capulets and move the setting from Italy to Appalachia and it's a Shakespearean-level bloodbath in the hills of eastern Kentucky.

First stop: the Pikeville-Pike County Visitors Center to pick up the audio CD or USB for the driving tour—a full-on feud immersion with narration, music, and jaunty ballads about the long-running grudge match that had its roots in the Civil War. See grave sites of the feuding families' kinfolk, the sites of the "Cotton Top" Hanging, the McCoy Homeplace and Well, and the pawpaw trees—where the blood of a grisly triple murder once stained the ground.

Plan to spend four to six hours immersed in the stories of these gun-wielding vigilantes who shot the world's most famous feud straight into the history books.

**TIP:** The **Hatfield McCoy Heritage Days** takes place annually in mid-September.

McCoy grave site, Hatfields & McCoys Historic Feud Sites/ Driving Tour (Courtesy of Kathryn Witt)

The Overlook at the Pikeville Cut-through (Courtesy of Pikeville-Pike County Tourism CVB)

# Pikeville Cut-through/ Overlook

Bob Amos Dr. • 606-432-5063
tourpikecounty.com

☑ Picnic, paddle, and saddle high above Pikeville. Bob Amos Park is located atop the Pikeville Cut-through on Peach Orchard Mountain, where sweeping vistas of the valley show off the results of the largest engineering feat in the United States, second in the world only to the Panama Canal.

Eighteen million cubic yards of earth were moved during the project to relocate a four-lane highway, railroad, and river through the mountain. Called the eighth wonder of the world, the Cut-through offers adventure aplenty on the mountain, including guided horseback riding (beginner to advanced), as well as kayaking, canoeing, and paddleboating on the Levisa Fork of the Big Sandy River.

Pack a picnic or pick up sandwiches, salads, and fresh-baked cake from **Mona's Restaurant** in Pikeville. If the only thing you do is lounge at the Overlook and drink in that spectacular tableau, it is time well spent.

# Chirico's Ristorante

235 Main St. • 606-432-7070 • facebook.com/chiricosristoranteky

☑ Randolph McCoy slept here.

Old Ranel himself, patriarch of the McCoy clan, once strode upon these floorboards and slipped out onto the second-floor balcony to contemplate Dils Cemetery yonder, where he had buried his wife, Sarah, and their daughter, Roseanna.

Today, the former McCoy House, a stop on the Feud driving tour, is Chirico's Ristorante. Dine on authentic Italian dishes, from classic favorites like the Italian sampler starter—featuring hand-rolled meatballs and scratch-made Italian sausage—to house specialties including the traditional Frankwich. Part sandwich, part pizza, this Chirico's original is layered with ham, pepperoni, mozzarella, and zesty cheeses, baked in a brick oven, and finished with lettuce, tomato, and mayo.

Place your order, then head up to the second floor, ascending the same staircase Randolph and Sarah walked up each night until their respective deaths. The McCoys moved here in 1888, after their Pike County Homeplace was burned to the ground by the Hatfields during the New Year's Day raid of that year.

Chirico's Ristorante (Courtesy of Kathryn Witt)

## Nearby Alternatives

### Outdoors: Jenny Wiley State Resort Park

Enjoy a morning paddle on **Dewey Lake** or an afternoon of fishing off its banks. Watch 700-pound elk roam freely on reclaimed land during a guided elk-viewing tour (September through March) or hike the **Lakeshore Hiking Trail** in search of bald eagles. Like fried catfish? The park's **Music Highway Grill** is famous for this dish served with hush puppies.
**75 Theatre Ct., Prestonsburg 606-889-1790, parks.ky.gov**

### Outdoors: Sugarcamp Mountain Trails

By foot, wheel, or hoof, this multiuse trail system in the mountains of eastern Kentucky throws everything it has at hikers, bikers, and horseback riders, including spectacular views of Dewey Lake—rugged terrain, varying levels of difficulty, and for mountain bikers, rock jumps, tabletops, zigzags and switchbacks, bridges, and boulders.
**Sugarcamp Mountain Rd. Prestonsburg, 606-886-1341**
sugarcamptrails.com

### Historic Venue: Mountain HomePlace

Practice the three Rs—reading, writing, and 'rithmetic—in the one-room schoolhouse at this living history museum representing life in 1850s rural Appalachian Kentucky. Lead the congregation in a hymn, weave cloth, watch a blacksmith forge a tool, attend a concert, feed goats—and listen as John Boy Walton (Johnson County's own Richard Thomas) narrates the museum's video.
**445 Kentucky Rte. 2275 Staffordsville, 606-297-1850**
paintsvilletourism.com

### Outdoors: Buckhorn Lake State Resort Park

Got horseshoes? Toss a ringer at the park's horseshoe pits. Play miniature golf, swim and splash in the lake, or sun on the sandy beach. Hike the **Moonshine Trail**, see a tribute in the lodge to the once-flourishing community of Bowlingtown, and dig into soup beans and corn bread in the park's **Bowlingtown Country Kitchen**.
**4441 Kentucky Hwy. 1833 Buckhorn, 606-398-7510**
parks.ky.gov

## Trip Planning

**Pikeville-Pike County Visitors Center**
**831 Hambley Blvd. Pikeville, 606-432-5063**
tourpikecounty.com

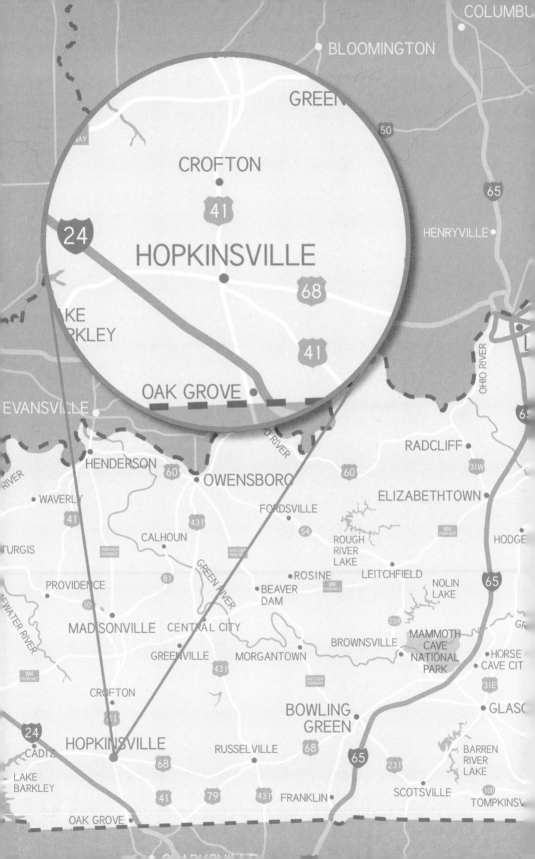

# HOPKINSVILLE

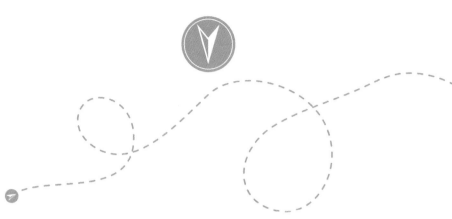

**S**TANDING 11 FEET TALL and weighing a whopping 1,500 pounds, the world's largest wheat stalk proclaims to all who come to downtown Hopkinsville that they have arrived in the Batter Capital of the World.

Kentucky's leading wheat-producing county, which annually harvests over 3,000,000 bushels of wheat from 46,200 acres of farmland, offers plenty of ways to experience the theme: queue up behind the giant Batter Bowl in the visitors center (hello, selfie!); whet your appetite at the giant, buttery Pancake Stack on display at the Pennyroyal Area Museum; pick up a skillet boasting, "Batter Capital of the World," the bestseller in the Visitor Center gift shop; or stop by a Hoptown restaurant for a signature wheat-based specialty recipe.

Against a rural backdrop, the Hopkinsville Historic District shows off ornate architecture housing a variety of businesses, including the circa-1928 landmark Alhambra Theatre and lots of locally owned specialty shops and restaurants. On downtown's outskirts, sit on one of the 24 stone seats encircling King Arthur's Round Table at Round Table Literary Park or tug on the sword in the stone.

# Pennyroyal Scuba Center Blue Springs Resort

602 Christian Quarry Rd. • 270-887-2585 • pennyroyalscuba.com

✓ Dinosaurs. Penny the Shark. A bathtub. See these sunken treasures and more at depths of five to 120 feet when you dive into the spring-fed, clear-blue waters of this 22-acre rock quarry. Kentucky's only full-service, diver-exclusive facility also harbors a UFO, a Cessna wreck, a 1941 Dodge Firetruck, and Big and Little Forests among more than three dozen lures.

Divers from beginner through advanced can practice their skills, complete certification dives, and enjoy this underwater world filled with marine life and perhaps an errant pirate's skeleton or two. Friday and Saturday night dives are available—the best times to spot catfish and crayfish (aka freshwater lobster).

Except for hoods and gloves (both available for purchase), the scuba center rents most items divers need, or divers may bring their own gear.

**TIP:** The resort offers primitive camping and a limited number of RV hookups, plus changing house and concession stand.

Pennyroyal Scuba Center Blue Springs Resort (Courtesy of Visit Hopkinsville)

Trail of Tears Intertribal Pow Wow at the Trail of Tears
Commemorative Park (Courtesy of Tommy Lopez)

# Trail of Tears Commemorative Park | 100 Trail of Tears Dr. • 270-886-8033
trailoftearshopkinsville.org

✓ These peaceful and lushly landscaped grounds on the banks of the Little River belie the tragedy that unfolded here in 1838 during the forced removal of Native Americans from their homelands. The grounds served as the winter camp for the Cherokee people on their way to Oklahoma.

The first stop on the Trail of Tears National Historic Trail, which extends through 10 states, designated a Trail of Tears National Park Site by President Ronald Reagan in 1987, it encompasses the Trail of Tears Commemorative Park and Heritage Center. The accessible center is tucked in a restored 19th-century log cabin and filled with Native American artifacts—a Bible written in Cherokee among the items.

Also here are two of the few known and verified grave sites on the trail—the final resting place of Chiefs White Path and Fly Smith. Explore the statue garden, flag memorial, and woodland path.

TIP: The Trail of Tears Intertribal Pow Wow, with dance and drum competitions, vendors, and arts and crafts, is held annually the first weekend after Labor Day.

# Ferrell's Snappy Service

1001 S Main St. • 270-886-1445

☑ If nostalgia had a flavor it would taste like sautéed onions on a sizzling burger, seasoned with pinches of salt and pepper and dripping with melty cheese.

Not fancy but very friendly, this tiny eight-stool Hoptown treasure with iconic neon sign has been serving burgers, breakfast, and chili for nearly 90 years. Hugging a corner downtown, the hut-sized eatery with old-school diner vibe is considered a Kentucky landmark and a must-visit for anyone coming to Hopkinsville.

Plan to order to go. The line sometimes gets long, but that only means the food is worth the wait. Grab a barstool if you can and watch the magic happen on Ferrell's well-seasoned grill. This is authentic mom-and-pop burger joint cookin' at its best.

Ferrell's (Courtesy of Visit Hopkinsville)

## Nearby Alternatives

**Distillery:** Casey Jones Distillery

Al Capone, axe-wielding revenuers, square pot stills built for quick getaways, and a legendary bootlegger who did jail time. The story of Casey Jones—the man, the master stillmaker, and the distillery—is carried on by Jones's grandson at this Kentucky Bourbon Trail Craft Tour® distillery that honors him with authentic small-batch moonshine and bourbon.

**2815 Witty Ln., 270-839-9987**
caseyjonesdistillery.com

**Outdoors:** Viceroy Butterfly Garden

Flutters of butterflies flit about this haven, a Certified Monarch Waystation and place of peace and reflection for visitors, with gazebo and Adirondack chairs set amid fields of sunflowers and other colorful, sun-loving blooms. See 1,800 butterflies take flight during Oak Grove's September Butterfly Festival.

**101 Walter Garret Ln.**
**Oak Grove, 270-439-5675**
visitoakgroveky.com

**Outdoors:** Mantle Rock Nature Preserve

This natural refuge is home to rare and fragile sandstone glades, riots of springtime wildflowers, and a thickly canopied upland forest, anchored by a 30-foot-high sandstone bridge spanning nearly 190 feet. A certified site on the Trail of Tears National Historic Trail, its hallowed grounds echo with the footfalls of the Cherokee Nation.

**Mantle Rock Rd., Smithland**
**859-259-9655**
nature.org/en-us/get-involved/how-to-help/places-we-protect/mantle-rock-preserve

**Outdoors:** Pennyrile Forest State Resort Park

Here is the complete family vacation: swimming and sandy beach; canoeing, kayaking, pedal boating—even standup paddleboarding—on Pennyrile Lake; 18-hole golf course, miniature golf course, horseshoes, hiking, fishing, picnicking, and horseback riding on trails in surrounding Pennyrile State Forest. A beautiful stone lodge with restaurant and guest rooms plus cabins and campground.

**20781 Pennyrile Lodge Rd.**
**Dawson Springs, 270-797-3421**
parks.ky.gov

## Trip Planning

Hopkinsville-Christian County Convention & Visitors Bureau
**1730 E 9th St., 270-887-2300**
visithopkinsville.com

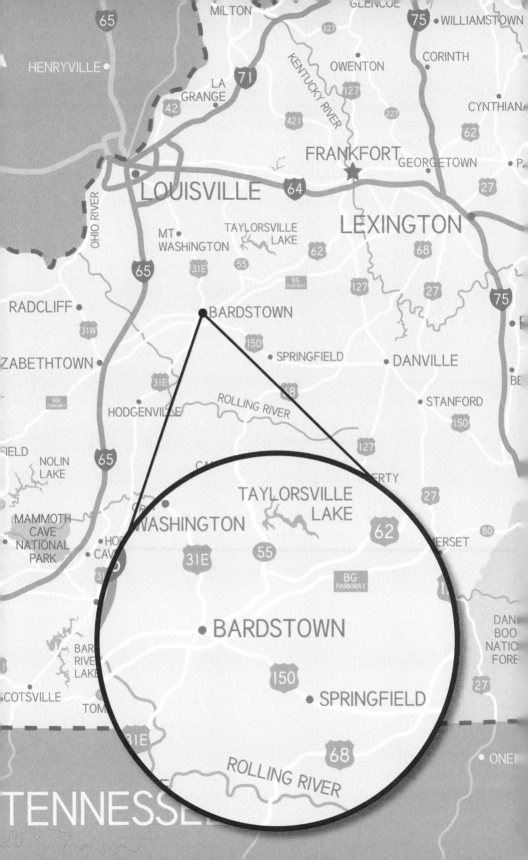

# BARDSTOWN

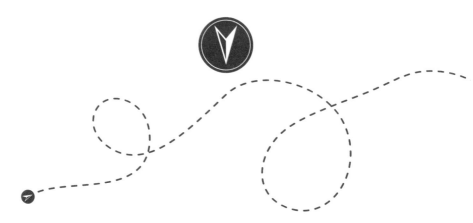

**C**ONSIDERED ONE OF America's most beautiful small towns, Bardstown is also the Bourbon Capital of the World and an Official Gateway to the famed Kentucky Bourbon Trail. With more than 10 unique distillery experiences in and around Bardstown (and all within about 15 miles of downtown's Court Square), Bardstown is the bourbon afficionado's nirvana.

Spirits of the haunted variety may be experienced at the oldest Western stagecoach stop in America—Talbott Tavern, built in 1779 and today a restaurant, bourbon bar, and inn. And the spirit will surely move you at the Basilica of St. Joseph Proto, the first Catholic cathedral west of the Allegheny Mountains.

Stroll through the colonial settlement at Historic Bardstown Village en route to Museum Row and the Civil War Museum and Women's Museum of the Civil War. See drummer boys' drums, surgical field kits, diaries, and other memorabilia, and learn about the roles women performed, including soldier and spy.

Bardstown is also known far and wide as one of Kentucky's most Christmassy towns. With its towering, twinkling Christmas tree at Court Square, illuminated lampposts trimmed with greenery, parade, decorated storefronts, and trains chugging to the "North Pole," it could be the setting for a holiday movie from a certain well-known channel.

# Kentucky Bourbon Trail®

kybourbontrail.com

☑ The best place to begin a quest is at the beginning. With a 5,000-piece collection spanning pre-Colonial days to post-Prohibition years, the Oscar Getz Museum of Whiskey History (114 N Fifth St.) is ideal prepping for touring and exploring (and tasting the bourbon at) the legendary distilleries on this well-trod trail, which has cultivated more than 45 superlative and immersive bourbon experiences. Discover bourbon's backstory among exhibits including Abraham Lincoln's tavern license, Prohibition-era "prescriptions," and an authentic moonshine still.

You know the names: Heaven Hill, Jim Beam, Maker's Mark, Four Roses, Angel's Envy, Evan Williams, Wild Turkey . . . With more than three dozen world-famous and not-to-be-missed distilleries on the trail, planning is essential. Fortunately, step-by-step trip planners help bourbon lovers map out the trail they want to blaze by distillery, location, date, transportation (guided, chauffeured, boat, bike), and adventure, like **Hartfield & Co.'s** Day as a Distiller or Build Your Own Old Fashioned at **Hermitage Farm**.

Heaven Hill Bourbon Experience (Courtesy of Visit Bardstown)

*The Stephen Foster Story* at My Old Kentucky Home State Park (Courtesy of Visit Bardstown)

# My Old Kentucky Home State Park "The Stephen Foster Story"

501 E Stephen Foster Ave. • 502-348-3502
visitmyoldkyhome.com

America's first pop star rocks the stage during *The Stephen Foster Story*, Kentucky's official outdoor musical and its longest-running outdoor drama. Sing along to timeless tunes like "Camptown Races" and "My Old Kentucky Home." See dozens of colorful, spinning skirts; hear the jaunty rattle of the tambourine; and watch a full-scale replica paddle wheel glide onto the stage. A second main-stage production (typically a family-friendly musical) gives visitors a chance to see two different but equally appealing productions.

The shows take place in My Old Kentucky Home State Park, in sight of My Old Kentucky Home, the stately 200-year-old manse known as Federal Hill. Tragedy, duels, tales of fame and fortune—hear about the house's history while wandering among fine antiques original to the home. Take a guided tour that concludes with the singing of the state anthem or come for an event: a ghost tour, a program about Victorian mourning and funerary customs, or outstanding drama/tour, "An Old Kentucky Christmas Carol."

# Kitchen & Bar at Bardstown Bourbon Company

1500 Parkway Dr. • 502-233-4769 • bardstownbourbon.com

☑ Bourbon tours and tastings plus temptations aplenty. Dine on classic fare infused with hometown flavors—pan-seared Verlasso salmon succulent in an apple cider–bourbon glaze and a bacon burger made with Kentucky-raised beef and topped with Benedictine. The cucumber-and-cream-cheese spread, spiced with onion and hot pepper and traditionally tinted green with food coloring, was invented by Louisville caterer Jenny Benedict in the early 20th century.

The bright, airy atmosphere entices with comfortable gathering spaces and an extensive bourbon menu. Be prepared for the chef to woo you right from the start(ers), with tasty bites like Kentucky poutine, beans and corn bread, and country ham with bourbon grains—all featuring locally sourced ingredients.

The restaurant calls itself "the first Napa Valley–style destination on the **Kentucky Bourbon Trail**® to combine distilling, culinary, and beverage expertise to create a modern, authentic bourbon experience." We call it a full-on culinary delight.

Kitchen & Bar at Bardstown Bourbon Company (Courtesy of Visit Bardstown)

# Nearby Alternatives

## Restaurant/Excursion Train: My Old Kentucky Dinner Train

Trundle through Bernheim Forest aboard a period-restored vintage train while lunching, dining, or sleuthing out whodunit. The dining is fine (seasonally inspired menus), the views are spectacular, and the experience is pure nostalgic fun. Signature menu items include Golden Spike Salad with secret-recipe dressing and Chocolate Choo-Choo with Chantilly cream and dark chocolate mousse.

**602 N 3rd St.**
**502-348-7300**
**kydinnertrain.com**

## Accommodations: Bourbon Manor Bed & Breakfast

When in Rome . . . Book the Mint Julep, one of 10 spirits-themed, luxury-level, antique-laden guest rooms at the country's first bourbon-themed B and B. Wake to an award-winning country gourmet breakfast (bourbon-infused French toast, anyone?). Unwind during a couples massage. Gardens, bourbon bar, and gift shop complete this picture of paradise for bourbon lovers.

**714 N 3rd St.**
**502-309-2698**
**bourbonmanor.com**

## Outdoors: Bernheim Arboretum and Research Forest

Scamper among treetops on a Canopy Tree Walk 75 feet above the forest floor. Meet genial goliaths Mama Loumari, Little Elina, and Little Nis—recycled wood sculptures. Hike and bike the trails. Dig in the sand pit at Playcosystem, a natural playground. Climb the fire tower—up, up, up 961 feet for incredible views.

**2075 Clermont Rd., Clermont**
**502-955-8512**
**bernheim.org**

## Behind-the-Scenes Tour: Kentucky Cooperage

Watch skilled craftsmen assemble seasoned staves to build the barrels that hold and age Kentucky bourbon. See the barrels enter the char box and get flame-licked to perfection, ready to impart spicy notes, vanilla flavors, and rich, beautiful color. Tours: 9 a.m., 10:30 a.m., and 1 p.m. Monday through Friday.

**711B E Main St., Lebanon**
**270-402-8009**
**kentuckycooperagetours.com**

# Trip Planning

**Visit Bardstown**
**1 Court Square**
**502-348-4877**
**visitbardstown.com**

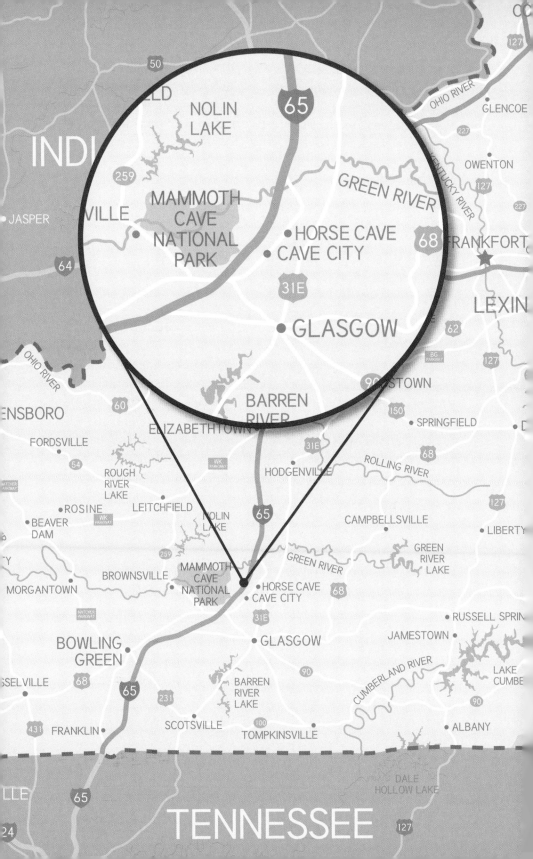

# HORSE CAVE & MAMMOTH CAVE

**L**ONGEST CAVE SYSTEM in the world at Mammoth Cave: check. Longest underground suspension bridge at Hidden River Cave: check. One of the few caves in the world located directly beneath a town—again, Hidden River Cave—housing one of the largest free-standing cave domes, and with an entrance right on Main Street. Check, check, and check.

Kentucky Cave Country is all about the superlative experience. And not just underground.

Horse Cave has animal encounters, free bluegrass jam sessions at the historic Thomas House, and lots of outdoor adventures. Rappel down the face of Hidden River Cave. Play disc golf and paddleball at Green River Park & Arboretum. Wander among mysterious rock formations at Kentucky Stonehenge in nearby Munfordville.

At Mammoth Cave National Park, paddle the Green and Nolin Rivers Blueway—Kentucky's first National Water Trail—to Bridal Veil Falls. Hike, bike, or horseback ride over 80 miles of trails. Fish, camp, canoe, or kayak. Go birding on a ranger-led program or join in a ranger-led discussion on the plants, animals, history, and geology above and below ground.

# Mammoth Cave National Park

1 Mammoth Cave Pkwy., Mammoth Cave
270-758-2180 • nps.gov/maca

✓ Each year over two million people visit the Mother Cave—Kentucky's oldest tour attraction and, at 426 explored miles, the world's longest known cave system. A UNESCO World Heritage Site, an International Biosphere Reserve, a certified International Dark Sky Park (*the* place for stargazing), home to the Green and Nolin Rivers Blueway—Mammoth Cave is an overachiever that lives up to its name.

Visit the **Old Guide's Cemetery**. Share a picnic on the banks of the Green River. Walk through the rock layers and see the earth's formation up close in a place that is as old as the prehistoric seas of the Mississippian Era.

Go underground like the cave's early explorers did, with only the light of a lantern to guide your steps over steep hills and uneven terrain. Tour the **Giant's Coffin**. Cross the River Styx. See stone huts where 19th-century tuberculosis patients checked in for treatment.

**TIP:** See the historic and restored 19th-century Mammoth Cave Stagecoach on permanent display at the refurbished Lodge at Mammoth Cave.

Mammoth Cave National Park (Courtesy of NPS Photo)

Hidden River Cave (Courtesy of Horse Cave/Hart County Tourist Commission)

# Hidden River Cave/American Cave Museum

119 E Main St., Horse Cave
270-786-1466 • hiddenrivercave.com

Home of the American Cave Conservation Association, this free-admission museum tells the story of the pollution that clogged Hidden River Cave for decades until a massive clean-up restored it to treasured landmark status. The self-guided tour features exhibits about karst geology, a landscape characterized by sinkholes, sinking streams, caves, and springs, as well as the archaeology of caves.

The museum sits at Main Street level. Look down far below: the entrance of Hidden River Cave yawns at the bottom of a 200-plus-step descent. Inside, grand-scale drama awaits.

The world's longest underground suspension bridge swings high above the river rushing below. Hang onto the handrails as you cross to the other side with the tour guide, and to the cave's pièce de résistance: Sunset Dome. At five acres, it is one of the largest freestanding cave domes in the United States. It's beautiful, too, soaring 100 feet high and burnished in shades of red, yellow, and orange.

# Farmwald's Restaurant and Bakery

3720 L&N Turnpike, Horse Cave
270-786-5600 • farmwalds.com

☑ Don't be surprised if you see horse-drawn buggies hitched in downtown Horse Cave and clip-clopping along the county's rural roads. Horse Cave has a large—and growing—Amish population and a thriving Amish business landscape.

It is one that Farmwald's fits right into, a rambling building in a cheery, country store setting. This Amish-owned eatery, open for breakfast and lunch, is known for its freshly baked doughnuts, breads, and melt-in-your-mouth fried pies, along with chicken baskets, fish dinners, and made-to-order deli lunches where you can build-your-own cold-cut sandwich. Sweet treats include small-batch, homemade ice cream.

A gift shop stretches across one side of the building, shelves brimming with local honey and jarred condiments, wooden toys and woven baskets, home decor, and accessories—mostly made by craftspeople from the local Amish community. A fireplace and cozy seating group add warmth and help make shoppers feel right at home.

Farmwald's Restaurant and Bakery (Courtesy of Horse Cave & Hart County Tourist Commission)

## Nearby Alternatives

### Animal Encounters: Kentucky Down Under Adventure Zoo; Dutch Country Safari Park

Traverse the wilds of Kentucky backcountry to pet (or nap with) kangaroos, see animal shows, mine for gemstones, and explore cave cauliflower at Mammoth Onyx Cave at the Kentucky Down Under Adventure Zoo; feed Watusi cattle, water buffalo, camels, and wildebeests that nose into the hay wagon at Dutch Country Safari Park.

**3700 L&N Turnpike, Horse Cave, 270-786-1010**
kentuckydownunder.com
**2125 L&N Turnpike Horse Cave, 270-925-4417**
kygetaway.com/dutch-country-safari-park

### Campground: Horse Cave KOA Holiday

Climb into the treetops for cozy overnights in a treehouse. Crawl into a Conestoga wagon or slip into a custom-built teepee, each with private patio and firepit. Clean, comfortable, and overlooking gently rolling pastureland, the campground also offers a beautifully maintained bathhouse, plus fishing pond and seasonal swimming pool.

**489 Flint Ridge Rd., Horse Cave 270-786-2819**
kygetaway.com/horse-cave-koa-holiday

### Outdoors: Dinosaur World

Think Jurassic Park without the rampaging velociraptors. Thickly forested wilderness. Paved walking paths. Stegosaurus, triceratops, dilophosaurus—even T. rex—and dozens and dozens of their behemoth brethren stomp about in open-air natural settings. A dinosaur-themed playground, fossil dig, gift shop, and picnic areas round out a fun family adventure.

**711 Mammoth Cave Rd. Cave City, 270-773-4345**
dinosaurworld.com

### Underground: Crystal Onyx Cave

Descend the stairs into this family-owned show cave, established in 1960 and rich in speleothem (formations): cave popcorn, dripping domes, stalactites, stalagmites, sinkholes, cave drapery, and rimstone dams. Dress for 58 degrees and bring your camera. Each half-mile guided tour is an original. Open March through December.

**425 Prewitts Knob Rd., Cave City 270-773-3377**
crystalonyxcaveky.com

## Trip Planning

### Horse Cave & Hart County Tourist Commission

**P.O. Box 385, Horse Cave 270-218-0386**
kygetaway.com

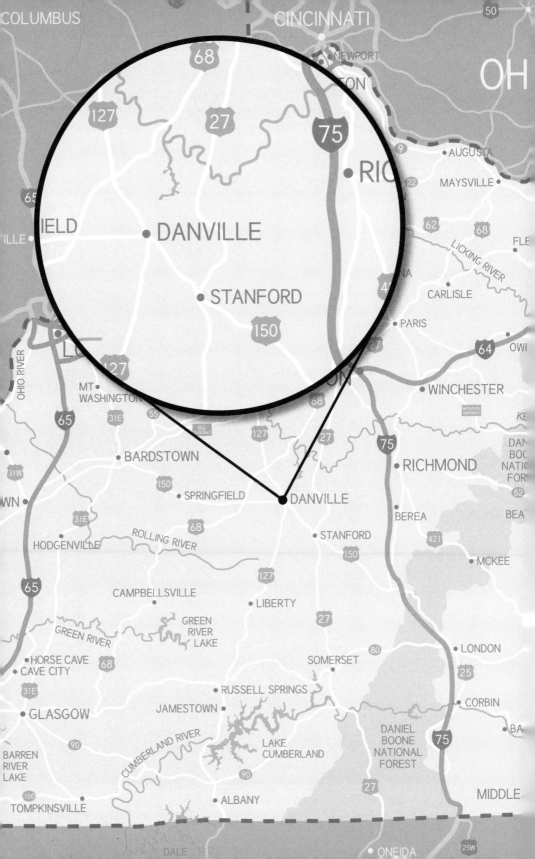

# DANVILLE

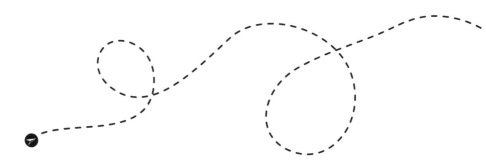

**I**T MAY BE be surprising that this small-town charmer is home to one of the country's largest bourbon distilleries. But it is. Wilderness Trail Distillery, a founding distillery destination on the Kentucky Bourbon Trail Craft Tour® and a stop on the Kentucky Bourbon Trail®, has a world-class facility and is fearless in making its mark on bourbon's ever-changing landscape.

It is perfectly in step with a town that proclaims itself "historically bold." Known as the City of Firsts, Danville claims the first post office west of the Allegheny Mountains, first courthouse in Kentucky, and first state school for the deaf. The capital of the Kentucky District of Virginia and of the new Commonwealth of Kentucky (for three days), Danville is where Kentucky statehood began.

With the circa 1700s log houses of Constitution Square Historic Site and a vibrant arts scene—one filled with contemporary public art and anchored by the Norton Center for the Arts and the new GLASS National Art Museum, featuring internationally known hot-glass master of color Stephen Rolfe Powell—Danville is both living history museum and open-air art gallery.

# Great American Dollhouse Museum

344 Swope Dr. • 859-236-1883
thedollhousemuseum.com

☑ See reality shrunk down at the only museum dedicated to chronicling in miniature the social history of the United States.

Explore more than 200 dollhouses and room boxes—artisan, antique, contemporary, historical—animated with tiny people and furnishings and rich in detail, color, and humor. Each piece tells a story along a timeline from the Native American and Colonial eras, through the Civil War and Old West chapters of American history, to life in the 20th century.

Visit **Alma's Farm Road**, a 1910 rural display complete with blacksmith, apple-juicing equipment, and country doctor. Encounter townsfolk and farmers, mischief-makers, and busybodies—the everyday people who make up a neighborhood. See fashions, tastes, technologies, and communities change and evolve.

In the **Dorothy Johnson Henry Dollhouse**, see an extraordinary collection of artists' miniatures. Enter an elaborate medieval quest story at the 14th-century Mummert's Castle at Martha's Mill. Shop the Miniatures Store, brimming with everything both miniaturist collector and hobbyist need.

Great American Dollhouse Museum (Courtesy of Danville-Boyle County Convention and Visitors Bureau)

Pioneer Playhouse (Courtesy of Pioneer Playhouse)

# Pioneer Playhouse

840 Stanford Rd. • 859-236-2747 • pioneerplayhouse.com

✓ Walk past the box office, which was the original train station from *Raintree County*, the 1957 MGM movie classic starring Elizabeth Taylor, and into Kentucky's oldest outdoor theater. It was founded in 1950 by a visionary who dreamt of bringing Broadway to the bluegrass, and more than seven decades of history have been written on its stage.

Owned and operated by the Henson family, it is a Kentucky Historic Landmark and time capsule of 1950s summer stock theater where John Travolta and Lee Majors once performed.

Hear the ringing of the Old Danville Firehouse Bell: a delicious Kentucky farm-fresh dinner is served on the shaded patio and accompanied by live music. Take your seat under the stars and enjoy outstanding professional theater, including beloved Broadway comedies and musicals.

**TIP:** Plan time to stroll the **Antique Village**, peruse the exhibit on "The Making of *Raintree County*," and browse the **Kentucky Gallery**, a gift shop featuring artistic director Heather Henson's award-winning children's books.

# Copper and Oak

303 W Main St. • 859-209-2087 • copperandoakky.com

☑ In a small town that has built a reputation among foodies, this restaurant stands out as a place where people can come and lose time and themselves in an unforgettable dining experience.

Step inside to an upscale speakeasy atmosphere whose urban vibe is softened with honeyed hospitality. On the menu are craft burgers and beer, custom cocktails, and one outstanding bourbon selection. The bestseller? Kentucky Bourbon Trail® member Wilderness Trail, a distillery that focuses on a unique sweet mash process.

Menu favorites include the restaurant's locally sourced prime Black Angus steaks and dishes that add a twist on Southern favorites, like the hot honey chicken. A Sunday brunch pairs enticing entrées with bottomless mimosas and Bloody Marys.

**TIP:** A few sips of Wilderness Trail bourbon at Copper and Oak will likely inspire you to visit the distillery to tour and taste—and continue onward to other distilleries on the **Kentucky Bourbon Trail®**.

Copper and Oak (Courtesy of Danville-Boyle County Convention and Visitors Bureau)

## Nearby Alternatives

### Historic Site: Perryville Battlefield State Historic Site

Kentucky's bloodiest Civil War battle took place here on October 8, 1862. A museum, walking trails, guided tours, commemoration and reenactment events, and October Ghost Tours keep history alive. Recognized by the American Battlefield Trust as the "most intact battlefield of any major battle of the Civil War," Perryville is as haunted as Gettysburg.
**1825 Battlefield Rd. (KY 1920) Perryville, 859-332-8631**
parks.ky.gov

### Landmark Destination: Shaker Village of Pleasant Hill

Spend the night at what was once home to the United States' third-largest Shaker community. The country's largest private collection of original 19th-century buildings is a place of serenity and activity, with the Inn, heritage craft workshops, the **Trustees' Table restaurant**, 3,000-acre Nature Preserve, and special events.
**3501 Lexington Rd. Harrodsburg, 859-734-5411**
shakervillageky.org

### Outdoors: Old Fort Harrod State Park

At the first permanent settlement west of the Allegheny Mountains, climb the country's largest Osage orange tree. See a music box collection at Mansion Museum. Find souvenirs at the kid-friendly gift shop. See the Lincoln Marriage Temple and the faded tombstones at Pioneer Graveyard. Interpreters and pioneer-themed activities and events bring the park to life.
**100 S College St., Harrodsburg 859-734-3314**
parks.ky.gov

### Historic General Store: Penn's Store

Find penny candy and canned goods, an old coal stove and a cigar box "cash register"—even musicians pickin' and jammin' on weekends—at America's oldest country store in continuous ownership and operation by the same family. Rustic and weathered, it has stood the test of time since 1845.
**257 Penn's Store Rd. Gravel Switch, 859-332-7715**
facebook.com/profile.
php?id=100063601719686

## Trip Planning

**Danville-Boyle County Convention and Visitors Bureau**
**105 E Walnut St.**
**859-618-6433**
danvillekentucky.com

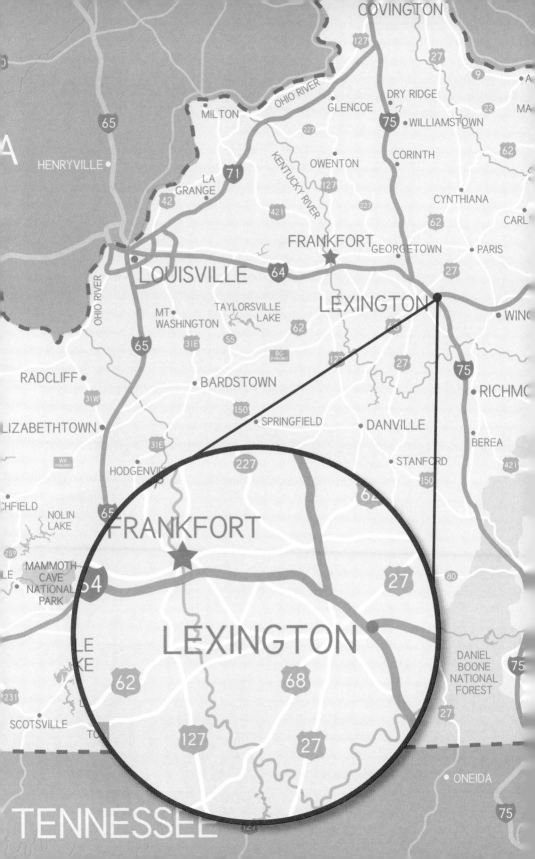

# LEXINGTON

**W**ITH MORE THAN 450 horse farms, world-class equine attractions, equine hospitals, racetracks, and feed mills—many of them situated on rolling countryside and framed by miles of blackwood paddock fencing—Lexington earns its place as the Horse Capital of the World.

See a herd of life-size bronze racehorses charging for the finish line in Thoroughbred Park and meet Kentucky Derby winners and other champion Thoroughbreds on dozens of different horse farm touring experiences, from independent to guided to chauffeured VIP tours.

Lexington is home to wineries, breweries, and distilleries, and a jumping-off point to more than a dozen area distilleries, including Versailles's architecturally distinctive Woodford Reserve and the James E. Pepper Distillery in the Historic Distillery District.

It is also steward to a pair of house museums—Ashland: the Henry Clay Estate and the Mary Todd Lincoln House—and a couple of quirky treasures: the Headley-Whitney Museum and its bibelots (small decorative baubles, ornaments, and other jeweled trinkets) and the Harry C. Miller Lock Collection with 12,000 safe locks in nearby Nicholasville.

# Kentucky Horse Park

4089 Iron Works Pike • 859-233-4303 • kyhorsepark.com

☑ This 1,200-acre everything-equine theme park—featuring live shows, multiple museums, and kid-friendly activities—celebrates humanity's relationship with the horse through education, exhibition, engagement, and competition. It is the only facility of its kind in the world.

Get immersed in horse history at the park's four museums: the **International Museum of the Horse**, a Smithsonian Affiliate, which examines the role of the horse from ancient times forward; the **Al-Marah Arabian Horse Galleries**, an especially delightful experience for pint-size explorers with interactive exhibits and a focus on Arabian horses; the **American Saddlebred Museum,** highlighting the "horse America made"; and the **Wheeler Museum**, with its collection of equestrian memorabilia.

Meet the horses that live in the park at the Hall of Champions, and during the Parade of Breeds Show and Stall-Side Chats at the Big Barn. Saddle up for trail rides and pony rides in the paddock. Overnight at the world-famous horse park at the campground equipped with swimming pool, sports courts, and other amenities.

Kentucky Horse Park (Courtesy of Kentucky Horse Park)

Keeneland (Courtesy of Kentucky Tourism)

# Keeneland

4201 Versailles Rd. • 859-254-3412 • keeneland.com

✓ Hear the horses' hooves pounding 'round the track during spring and fall meets in April and October.

A National Historic Landmark, the internationally renowned racecourse is known for the sheer beauty of its grounds; tailgate gatherings on "The Hill" with food trucks and Bluegrass music; and, among dining options, southern comfort-food breakfasts at the Track Kitchen, which presents the coveted opportunity to rub elbows with a who's who of horse jockeys and trainers.

Morning Workout Tours are available year-round. Special in-depth tours are available in April and October, including the Backstretch, Owner's Experience, and Behind-the-Scenes Racing.

Keeneland has starred as a setting for several high-profile movies, including the 2003 Oscar-nominated *Seabiscuit*; 2005's *Dreamer* with Kurt Russell; and *Secretariat*, the award-winning 2010 drama about the horse considered by many to be the greatest racehorse of all time.

**TIP:** Get to the **Keeneland Track Kitchen** early and participate in a Lexington tradition: watching the Thoroughbreds' morning workout following breakfast.

# Dudley's on Short

259 W Short St. • 859-252-1010 • dudleysonshort.com

☑ This iconic restaurant housed in the circa-1889 Northern Bank Building is a downtown Lexington landmark known for luscious dishes, a distinctive wine list, and a bar that inspires lingering conversation over classic cocktails. It is at once elegant and homey, a special-occasion restaurant or indulgent night out, with a gorgeous and warmly lit interior and peerless and intuitive service.

The menu is award-winning, refined American cuisine served with Dudley's own special flourish of inventiveness. From piled-high smoked Kentucky trout deviled egg starters to entrée classics like the mouthwatering Tournedos Maxwell, served with crabmeat and béarnaise, to sweet endings like the Bourbon Ball Cake, a chocolate cake frosted with bourbon buttercream—yes! bourbon buttercream—and topped with a bourbon ball, Dudley's is next-level dining.

Choose linen-draped dining inside the two-story restaurant or out on the patio, which also has cushioned couches arrayed amid the greenery. Either is a lovely backdrop for a memorable meal.

Dudley's on Short (Courtesy of VisitLEX)

## Nearby Alternatives

### Outdoors: Camp Nelson National Monument

Join a ranger-led tour of this federal army supply depot and hospital that became one of the largest recruitment and training centers for African American soldiers during the Civil War. Explore the Visitor Center and Museum, Grave No. 1 (Obelisk), and the five-mile trail system past infantry entrenchments and burial grounds.
**6614 Danville Rd. Loop 2 Nicholasville, 859-881-5716**
nps.gov/cane/index.htm

### Rail Excursion: Rail Explorers

Ride the rails through Thoroughbred farms, between limestone cliffs, to the Kentucky River at historic Young's High Bridge, and picture-postcard views of Wild Turkey Distillery, pedaling in tandem or quad on the "Rolls Royce of railbikes." Before or after, visit **Bluegrass Scenic Railroad & Museum** with model train exhibit and 90-minute excursions aboard an antique train.
**175 Beasley Rd., Versailles 877-833-8588**
railexplorers.net

### Restaurant/Accommodations: The Kentucky Castle

Book a royal getaway to a European-inspired castle complete with turrets, crenellated battlements, and lush grounds. Take a castle tour. Dine on magnificent farm-to-table meals. Sleuth your way through a murder mystery dinner. Indulge in a spa treatment. Overnight in your choice of accommodations—tiny home, castle room, tower suite (tiara add-on available).
**230 Pisgah Pike, Versailles 859-256-0322**
thekentuckycastle.com

### Shopping/Restaurant: Irish Acres Gallery and the Glitz

Wander through dozens of themed showrooms filled with artfully arrayed European and American antiques in a beautifully renovated 1930s school. Sit down to a three-course, *prix fixe* gourmet luncheon served in a fairy-tale setting at the restaurant hidden downstairs and glowing with twinkle lights. Open April through December with menus changing every three weeks.
**4205 Fords Mill Rd., Versailles 859-873-7235**
irishacresgallery.com

## Trip Planning

**VisitLEX Lexington Visitors Center**
**215 W Main St., Ste. 75 859-233-7299**
visitlex.com

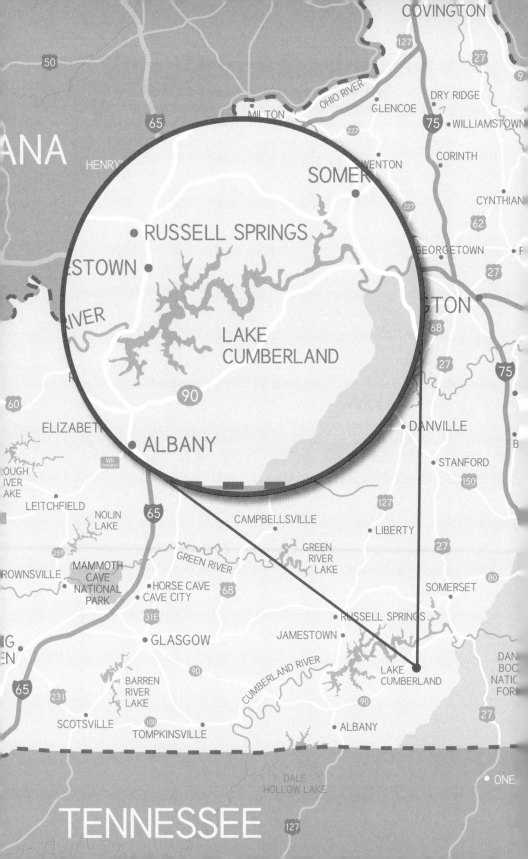

# LAKE CUMBERLAND & RUSSELL SPRINGS

**A**S THE GATEWAY to Lake Cumberland, one of the largest man-made lakes east of the Mississippi River, Russell Springs and surrounding communities serve up all the family fun and nostalgia one would expect to find at a laid-back lakeside vacation destination.

Places like Mini Indy Go Kart Track, Laker Lanes Bowling, and Player 1 Gaming—a shed filled with vintage items and knickknacks for gamers—provide fun on land. Shop Russell Springs' boutiques. Catch vintage cinema at the Historic Star Theater, an automobile garage turned movie theater. Golf 18 holes at Lakewood Country Club while the duffers in the group splash about the club's outdoor pool.

And then there is the lake. The towns within Russell County may feel mom-and-pop, but with most of Lake Cumberland lapping gently within its borders, there is big water fun and outdoor adventure to be had. Big. Huge. Five marinas, a skeet and trapshooting club, horseback trail rides, mountain bike trails, geocaching . . .

# State Dock Marina

6365 State Park Rd., Jamestown • 888-782-8336 • statedock.com

☑ Destination: the Houseboat Capital of the World. The itinerary? Lazy days aboard a houseboat tricked out with everything, including the kitchen sink (plus waterslides and hot tubs): playing watersports; fishing for striper; tying up at an island or hidden cove; creating lasting memories on a 60,000-acre lake surrounded by rugged beauty, stunning cliffs, plunging waterfalls, and as much shoreline as the entire state of Florida.

Choose your dream boat from a fleet of custom houseboats, each featuring private staterooms, equipped kitchen, outdoor seating, satellite television and music, party tops, and generously sized grills, and stocked with fresh linens, kitchen utensils—everything needed for a vacation to write home about.

Watercraft, including pontoons and tritoons—even a party barge—along with add-on gear like water skis, wakeboards, and tubes, add to the good times. As does a stop at the covered, nautical-themed **Boat Yard Bar and Grill**, serving breakfast, appetizers, hand-tossed pizza, burgers, milkshakes, and more (beer and mixed drinks, too), and accompanied by a party soundtrack.

State Dock Marina (Courtesy of Kentucky Tourism)

Lake Cumberland State Resort Park (Courtesy of Kentucky Tourism)

# Lake Cumberland State Resort Park

5465 State Park Rd., Jamestown
270-343-3111 • parks.ky.gov

✓ Check into **Lure Lodge** for breathtaking vistas of Lake Cumberland and settle onto your private balcony to catch a Kentucky sunset as it slips into the water. The park also has cottages sequestered in wooded settings as well as dozens of campsites, including RV and primitive sites.

Head outside for a day of hiking, disc golf, mini golf, tennis, swimming, geocaching—even 3D archery featuring life-size targets of deer, bear, and turkey. Downshift to a relaxing soak amid the bubbles at the hot tub located at the park's indoor pool complex, which also has a swimming pool.

Come fall, the park is ablaze with color, and leaf peepers can experience stunning pops of orange, red, and yellow from late September to early November. Fall also means astronomy programs with the park naturalist.

Whatever the season, enjoy the panoramic views from the lodge and **Rowena Landing Restaurant** and **Wake Zone**—a bar and grill within the restaurant.

# Coe's Steak House

2281 Lakeway Dr., Russell Springs • 270-866-9980
facebook.com/fishplace72

☑ Beloved by the locals, this small restaurant with an extra helping of heart has been dishing up rib eye, country ham, and crab cake dinners for half a century. Coe's most famous dish? In spite of its name, it is the fried catfish—hand-cut, freshly breaded, and fried to golden perfection, and served with hush puppies.

Dinner is nothing fancy, but it is something delicious with every mouthful and generous portions on every plate—from the appetizers, including tasty morsels like redneck tater skins and catfish bites, to the daily sides, country goodness like pintos, greens, and macaroni and cheese. Favorites among the homemade desserts are the coconut and chocolate pies, piled high with airy-sweet meringue.

Open Thursday through Saturday, Coe's is a highlight for many visitors to the lake—so popular it is standing room only at times. But that only proves how good the food is.

Coe's Steak House (Courtesy of Lake Cumberland Tourist Commission)

## Nearby Alternatives

### Outdoors: Wolf Creek National Fish Hatchery

Calling all families! Take an interactive walk through this pristine hatchery, or challenge yourself to a nature trail scavenger hunt. Venture outside to feed the trout or fish the cold-water trout stream. Hike **Whispering Pines Trail** or grab a snack from **Big Daddy's Eats & Treats** in Kendall Campground and play at the splash pad.

50 Kendall Rd., Jamestown
270-343-3797
fws.gov/fish-hatchery/wolf-creek

### Restaurant/Shopping: Campbell's Creelsboro Country Store

A general store built in 1876 and a hub for steamboats, this farm-to-table restaurant is a gathering space for hungry diners, shoppers browsing Kentucky-crafted products, and those seeking workshops in bread- and biscuit-making. Steps from the magnificent 60-foot-high limestone Creelsboro Natural Arch, an archway to the Cumberland River, the store also has kayak rentals available.

4838 S Hwy. 379, Jamestown
270-343-4277
campbellscreelsborocountrystore.com

### Outdoors: Dale Hollow Lake State Resort Park

Three thousand four hundred acres of forested hills, 620 miles of shoreline, and the still waters of Dale Hollow Lake dotted with islands equals one vacation paradise. The park's marina has a state-of-the-art facility, and the golf course is nationally ranked. Like adventure? Get wet and muddy on a guided wild cave tour at **Cindy Cave**.

5970 State Park Rd., Burkesville
270-433-7431
parks.ky.gov

### Outdoors: Haney's Appledale Farm

From roadside fruit stand to sprawling 400-acre farmland, this family-owned-and-operated farm is a southern Kentucky tradition. Shop for seasonal produce, sip freshly squeezed apple cider, bite into a fresh-from-the-oven fried pie, and stock up on salsas and sauces, jams and jellies, and more.

8350 Kentucky Hwy. 80, Nancy
606-636-6148
haneysappledalefarm.com

## Trip Planning

### Lake Cumberland Tourist Commission

650 South Hwy. 127, Russell Springs, 270-866-4333
lakecumberlandvacation.com

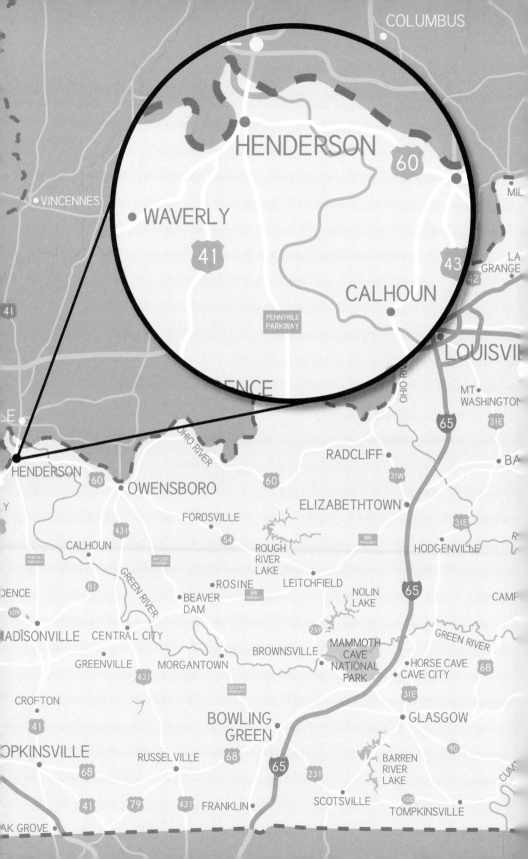

# HENDERSON

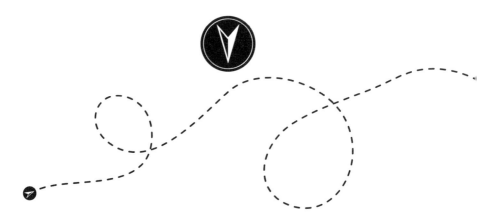

**J**OHN JAMES AUDUBON and W. C. Handy played here.

In fact, both pioneers in their respective fields spent about a decade of their lives in Henderson, living, learning, and pursuing their callings in wildlife artistry and blues music.

Find evidence of these historymakers in attractions like Audubon Mill Park, site of the annual W.C. Handy Blues & Barbecue Festival; a memorial sign dedicated to Handy within the park; and a self-guided Audubon Sculpture Walking Tour commemorating the naturalist and featuring 16 bronze sculptures, including one of the now-extinct passenger pigeon, wending through downtown.

Henderson's Historic Downtown District is a mix of architecturally enchanting homes and commercial buildings, bustling retail and restaurant landscape—emphasis on locally owned—and splashes of color, thanks to a series of vibrant murals, including one that invites visitors to discover their own nature. The theme is fitting given Henderson's peaceful riverfront setting with scenic walkway and fountains, a proliferation of parks, and the legacy of Audubon.

Stop by Butler's Apothecary for an ice cream from the old-fashioned soda fountain. Sip a wine slushie on the front porch at Boucherie Winery. During fall, visit Cates Farm & Produce to find the perfect pumpkin and navigate your way through a 15-acre corn maze.

# John James Audubon State Park and Museum

3100 US Hwy. 41 • 270-826-2247 • parks.ky.gov

☑ Spend time at this museum, housed in a beautiful stone château and displaying 200-plus artifacts, including one of the few existing copies of the rare double elephant folio edition of *Birds of America* (1827–1838), created by the legendary self-trained ornithologist, naturalist, and wildlife artist.

Explore the Audubon Wetlands, a 649-acre refuge for bald eagles, the great blue heron, woodpeckers, and waterfowl, which is reached by a boardwalk that overlooks the habitat and connects to more than six miles of hiking trails.

The Nature Center, located at the museum, has a wildlife observation room, Discovery and Learning Center, Audubon Theater, and exhibits of works by local artists. The gift shop stocks Audubon books, cards, and prints, as well as artisan-made, nature-inspired gifts, and (this being Kentucky), Kentucky Woods Bourbon Barrel Cakes.

Cottages and campsites are available for overnighting. **NOTE:** The **Ohio Valley Birding Festival** takes place at the park annually in April.

**TIP:** Once a month, on the first Wednesday or Thursday (before the doors of the museum are unlocked), the museum curator ceremoniously turns the pages of *Birds of America* to reveal different prints.

John James Audubon State Park and Museum
(Courtesy of Henderson Tourist Commission)

Ellis Park Racing & Gaming (Courtesy of Henderson Tourist Commission)

# Ellis Park Racing & Gaming

3300 Hwy. 41 N • 812-425-1456 • ellisparkracing.com

☑ There's nothing like sitting at the edge of your seat in the grandstand or hovering at the rail and watching Thoroughbred horses thunder past on their way to the finish line.

This Thoroughbred racetrack and casino has live Thoroughbred horse racing in the summertime and simulcast wagering all year long, plus 300 gaming machines—and a history that stretches back more than 100 years to 1922, when the land beneath the horses' hooves was nothing more than wet, scraggly river bottom.

Ellis Park is owned and operated by Churchill Downs, and the experience today is much different than those early years when the park was plagued by financial woes, flooding, and tornado damage—when the starting gate was pulled by mules and gamblers would arrive by ferry. A modern facility, fan-based experiences, a calendar filled with promotions, and breakfast and comfort food classics served at the **Dade Park Grill** make for a fun and exciting day at the races.

# Farmer & Frenchman Winery

12522 US Hwy. 41 S, Robards • 270-748-1856 • farmerandfrenchman.com

☑ Girlfriends, couples, and weekend wanderers are drawn to this small-farm vineyard, a complete destination with tastings, dining, solar-powered lodgings, events, and walking trails in an idyllic setting featuring sweeping views of farmland and surrounding countryside.

The family-owned winery blends the backgrounds of a Henderson local and a native of Paris, France, who craft wine the old-world way combined with state-of-the-art technology to capture varietal and regional character. The wine complements vineyard-to-table cuisine made with locally sourced ingredients.

The menu is seductive, showing off lavish Italian and French influences in dishes like duck confit and chicken scarpariello. Lighter fare like seafood a la plancha—a vibrant mélange of sautéed calamari and baby scallops, red bell pepper, garlic, onion, Spanish chorizo, and tomato sauce, delivers layers of flavor.

Of course, there is wine: Farmer and Frenchman's own—everything from sweet, white Dressed Up Farm Girl to dry, red old-vine zinfandel—along with wines from California, Italy, and France, and a variety of champagne.

Farmer & Frenchman Winery (Courtesy of Westmile Media)

## Nearby Alternatives

### Festival: W. C. Handy Blues & Barbecue Festival

Groundbreaking composer and Father of the Blues, William Christopher Handy spent a decade of his life in Henderson. His life and legacy are celebrated every year in mid-June during one of the nation's largest free music festivals. Come to Audubon Mill Park, overlooking the Ohio River, for four days of blues, barbecue, and beautiful views.

N Water St.
handyblues.org

### Venue: Preston Arts Center

Music, dance, drama, comedy—a variety of arts programming, including main stage and family shows, music concerts and community theater, takes place in this 951-seat lakeside theater located on the scenic Henderson Community College campus. Drop by the theater's gallery, where arts exhibits are hosted throughout the year.

2660 S Green St.
270-826-5916
pac.henderson.kctcs.edu

### Outdoors: Sloughs Wildlife Management Area

This 10,000-acre wildlife refuge with multiple observation towers, shelters, wetlands, and woodland habitats is recognized by the National Audubon Society as an Important Birding Area where more than 250 birds have been spotted. Kayak into an 1,800-acre cypress slough at Jenny's Hole to view bald eagles, wading birds, and waterfowl.

9956 KY-268, Corydon
270-827-2673
app.fw.ky.gov/Public_Lands_
Search/detail.aspx?Kdfwr_id=230

### Outdoors: Rough River Dam State Resort Park

Kentucky's smallest resort park is a quiet, scenic retreat with big fun: boating, beaching, and fishing for largemouth bass on Rough River Lake; playing disc golf on an 18-hole lakeside course; practicing navigational skills on the orienteering course; spotting bald eagles. Other amenities? There are an ADA-accessible marina, monthly bluegrass music nights, and summertime Friday night patio concerts.

450 Lodge Rd., Falls of Rough
270-257-2311
parks.ky.gov

## Trip Planning

### Henderson Tourist Commission

101 N Water St.
270-826-3128
hendersonky.org

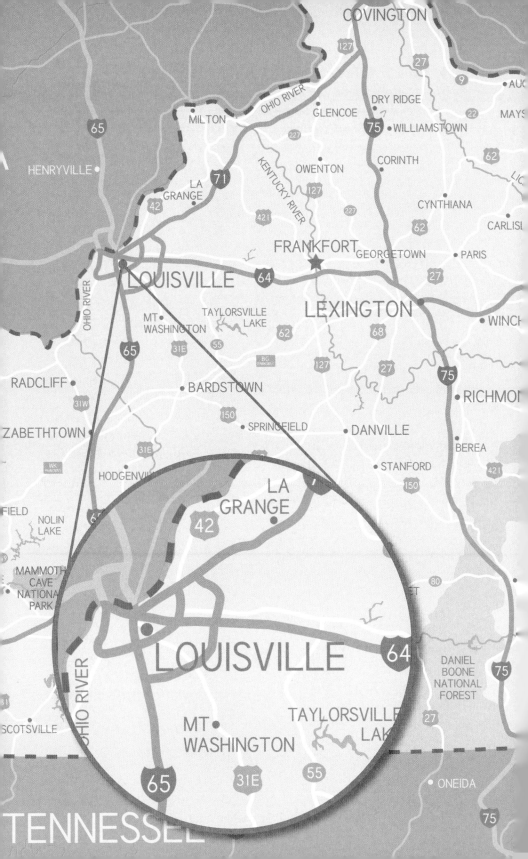

# LOUISVILLE

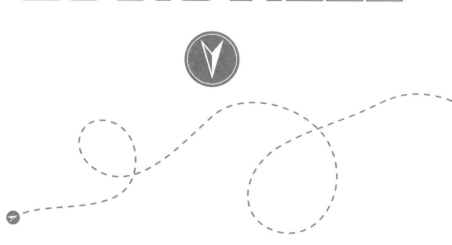

**L**OUISVILLE WEARS ITS Bourbon City nickname proudly as home to the only Urban Bourbon Trail®, a curated cocktail and culinary/bar and restaurant experience, and the official starting point of the Kentucky Bourbon Trail® at the Frazier History Museum. This Smithsonian Affiliate sits on Whiskey Row, crowded with both heritage distilleries like Old Forester and Evan Williams and bourbon upstarts like Rabbit Hole.

True, Louisville is awash in bourbon, but it is also a land of legends. America's only remaining authentic steamboat from the riverboat era, the grande dame herself—*Belle of Louisville*—is docked on Louisville's beautiful riverfront. Above is the historic Big Four Pedestrian Bridge at Waterfront Park, home of renowned artist Ed Hamilton's 12-foot sculpture of President Abraham Lincoln.

At the Louisville 21c Museum Hotel, a 30-foot-tall *David (inspired by Michelangelo)*, a golden replica of the marble original standing in Florence, Italy, ushers visitors into the boutique hotel's contemporary art gallery. Kentucky's oldest and largest art museum, the Speed, spans 6,000 years, from ancient Egypt to contemporary art. Louisville Mega Cavern yawns beneath the Louisville Zoo, offering zip lining and other underground adventures.

# Muhammad Ali Center

144 N 6th St. • 502-584-9254 • alicenter.org

✔ The life and legacy of the world heavyweight boxing champion, Olympic gold medalist, philanthropist, and activist is celebrated at this award-winning museum cofounded by Muhammad Ali and a stop on the US Civil Rights Trail.

Ali called himself "The Greatest" and was famous for his oft-quoted line—"Float like a butterfly, sting like a bee/The hands can't hit what the eyes can't see"—an inspiration to many who lived by six core principles: confidence, conviction, dedication, giving, respect, and spirituality. Visitors to the Ali Center experience these through multimedia and interactive exhibits and memorabilia, including *If You Can Dream*, an introductory film in the immersive five-screen Orientation Theater.

Shadow box with the Champ in the *Train with Ali* exhibit and find your rhythm on the speed bag. Watch historical interviews and video clips and footage of Ali bouts in the ring. See the torch Ali used to light the Olympic Cauldron at the 1996 Summer Games in Atlanta, Georgia.

Muhammad Ali Center (Courtesy of Muhammad Ali Center)

Louisville Slugger Museum & Factory (Courtesy of Kathryn Witt)

# Louisville Slugger Museum & Factory

800 W Main St. • 877-775-8443
sluggermuseum.com

☑ Adventure in America's National Pastime begins as soon as you spot the Big Bat, a 68,000-pound replica of Babe Ruth's 34-inch Louisville Slugger, rising 120 feet into the great blue yonder.

Enter the "Fort Knox of baseball bats," aka the Bat Vault, to see 3,000-plus original bat models—some more than 100 years old—designed by legendary baseball players. In the *Hold a Piece of History* exhibit, do exactly that: handle bats swung in baseball games by legends like Johnny Bench and Derek Jeter. Snap a selfie with life-size sculptures of baseball's big names: Hank Aaron, Babe Ruth, Roberto Clemente, Derek Jeter, Ken Griffey Jr., Jackie Robinson, and Ted Williams.

Go behind the scenes at the factory, following the bat-making process from forest to field. Smell the wood. Watch the wood chips fly. Learn the history of the company that has been making baseball bats since 1884. Climb the Big Glove, the centerpiece of the 17-ton "Play Ball" sculpture—and don't forget your free mini-bat souvenir.

# Jack Fry's

1007 Bardstown Rd. • 502-452-9244 • jackfrys.com

✓ From backroom bookmaking and bootleggin' to beloved cultural icon serving up a classic Louisville dining experience, this restaurant is named for its original owner—a gambler named Jack Fry, who gave this hangout a sportsman's ambience when he opened it in 1933.

Nine decades later, the restaurant has a solid reputation for above-and-beyond service, a warm and welcoming atmosphere heavy on nostalgia and with a speakeasy vibe, and American bistro fare with Southern influences. Escargots broiled in butter and shrimp and grits doused in red-eye gravy lead off a fine-dining menu of timeless favorites like grilled tenderloin, duck confit, local dry-aged chuck burger with caramelized onions, and grilled swordfish marinated and glazed with bourbon-smoked paprika and ancho-molasses.

Sweet treats, like a dark chocolate bombe and blood orange upside-down cake, show off the pastry chef's artistry. Live jazz, classic cocktails, and a wine list that puts a smile on the connoisseur's face round out the experience.

Jack Fry's (Courtesy of Jack Fry's)

# Nearby Alternatives

**Museum: Churchill Downs/Kentucky Derby Museum**

"The most exciting two minutes in sports." Bourbon-laced mint juleps. A parade of showy hats. And that song that makes Kentuckians cry, "The sun shines bright . . ." Yep. It's Churchill Downs, home of the Kentucky Derby, and the interactive Kentucky Derby Museum with exhibits, tours, and bourbon experiences.

**700 Central Ave., Louisville**
**502-636-4400**
churchilldowns.com

**Shopping: The Outlet Shoppes of the Bluegrass**

No need to pack your shopping shoes when you can find them among 20 footwear stores at Kentucky's only designer outlet shopping center with over 100 coveted shops and numerous restaurant choices. You know and love the brands: Tory Burch, Kate Spade, Yankee Candle, OshKosh B'gosh, Oakley, Fragrance Outlet.

**1155 Buck Creek Rd.**
**Simpsonville, 502-722-5558**
theoutletshoppesofthebluegrass.com

**Farm Tour/Restaurant/ Accommodations: Hermitage Farm**

Take a guided garden or Artwalk tour at this historic working Thoroughbred horse farm in Oldham County, the Farm Tour Capital of Kentucky. Sip Kentucky's finest bourbons at the **Bourbon Bar** and **Bourbon Library**. Dine farm-to-table in **Barn8**, tucked within a converted horse stable, and settle down for the night in luxurious accommodations.

**10500 W Hwy. 42, Goshen**
**502-398-9289**
hermitagefarm.com

**Outdoors: Yew Dell Botanical Gardens**

Step into this fairy-tale garden come to life, replete with turreted stone castle, for a magical day exploring more than a dozen themed gardens— Sunken Rock, Serpentine, Secret. The internationally recognized center of gardening, plants, and education is famous for its large and fanciful hellebore collection. Self-guided tours and events add to its allure.

**6220 Old LaGrange Rd.**
**Crestwood, 502-241-4788**
yewdellgardens.org

# Trip Planning

**Louisville Visitor Center**
**301 S 4th St.**
**888-568-4784**
gotolouisville.com

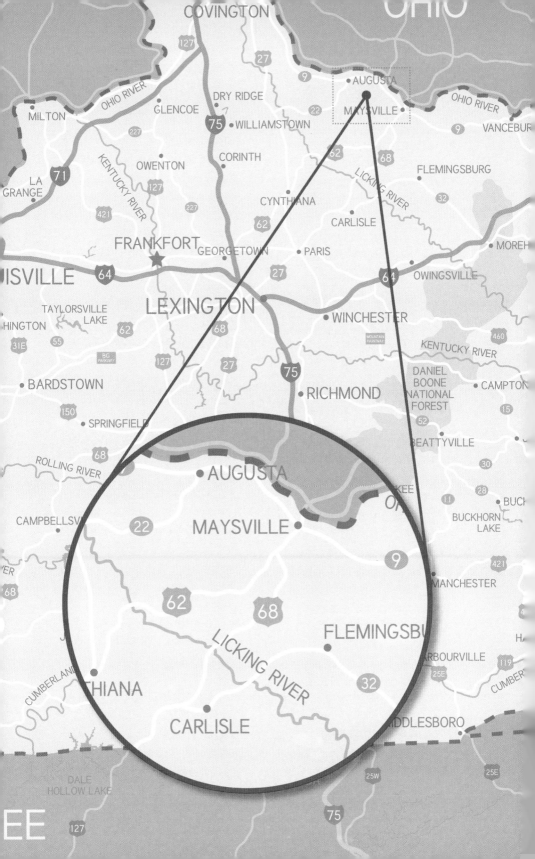

# MAYSVILLE & AUGUSTA

**M**AYSVILLE AND AUGUSTA may be separated by 20 miles, but they are linked by the charm of their scenic small-town settings on the banks of the Ohio River, the paddle-wheel boats that call at their ports, and one of Kentucky's most famous residents—singer-actress Rosemary Clooney, who was born in the former and lived for 22 years in the latter.

Maysville is bustling downtown shopping, centuries-old covered bridges, and Underground Railroad history—a story told through a richly detailed painting that is part of Maysville's Floodwall Murals created by world-renowned artist Robert Dafford. It is small-town picnics and parades and live productions at the fifth-oldest theater in the US—the Washington Opera Theatre, home to Kentucky's oldest theatrical group.

The "Most Picturesque Town in Kentucky," Augusta is that quiet weekend away at the end of a winding country road to explore an old-time general store, stroll along the riverbank past secret gardens and log cabins, and while away an afternoon at Rosemary Clooney's home, now a museum.

# The Old Pogue Distillery

705 Germantown Rd., Maysville • oldpogue.com

Beautifully situated on a bluff overlooking Maysville's Simon Kenton Bridge and Ohio River, the Old Pogue Distillery has a history stretching back about 150 years. It sits on the same grounds where the historic H.E. Pogue Distillery was located and drew its water and is operated by the fifth and sixth generations of the founding family using the original Pogue recipes and formula.

On the **Kentucky Bourbon Trail Craft Tour**® and a stop on **the B-Line**®—Northern Kentucky's bourbon trail of distilleries, bars, and restaurants—it is a history lesson about bourbon's beginnings and an homage to the bourbon-making tradition. Visitors find the historic home of the Pogue family—one of Kentucky's oldest whiskey families—as well as an artisan distillery, complete with tasting room, grain holding, and barrel storage.

**TIP:** The grounds of the Old Pogue Distillery are steep and enclosed by gates. Sixty-minute tours are available by appointment via the website.

The Old Pogue Distillery (Courtesy of Visit Maysville)

KSB Miniatures Collection at Kentucky Gateway Museum Center
(Courtesy of Kathryn Witt)

# Kathleen Savage Browning Miniatures Collection

Kentucky Gateway Museum Center • 215 Sutton St., Maysville
606-564-5865 • kygmc.org

A jolly baker lays out his ingredients. A ballerina in black feathers stands en pointe. The Evil Queen tempts Snow White while the Seven Dwarfs heigh-ho to the mines.

These treasures and others replicate in the most intricate detail the artistry of the miniaturist. Meticulously researched and exquisitey handcrafted, each fine art object in the seasonally changing collection is made using the same materials and techniques master artisans use on their full-size counterparts: 18th-century furniture, musical instruments, jewelry—even the tiniest rings are made from real gold and gemstones.

Guided tours (arranged by appointment) reveal galleries with both fantasy vignettes and historically accurate re-creations like Maysville's Russell Theatre. The early 1950s theater is rebuilt on a 1/12-inch scale using 11,000 hand-cut bricks. A highlight of the collection is Spencer House, Princess Diana's ancestral home.

**TIP:** Enjoy a tasting of Old Pogue Master's Select Bourbon and Old Maysville Club (fee) at the **Old Pogue Experience**, also located at the museum.

# Caproni's on the River

320 Rosemary Clooney St., Maysville
606-564-4321 • capronisontheriver.com

✓ A favorite of the Clooney family (as in Nick, Nina, Rosemary, and George), this iconic restaurant parked along the railroad tracks and overlooking the Ohio River has been in operation for nearly a century—since the 1930s, when it opened as a sandwich shop for railroad workers.

Those days are long gone, but the restaurant's welcoming ambience remains. With its warm brick-and-wood interior, a wall of windows framing a river vista, a brick beer garden, and the chummy, locally made cherrywood bar serving up classic cocktails, it's no wonder that locals and movie stars alike seek it out.

The menu shows off Kentucky culinary heart and soul: that cheesy sensation, the Hot Brown; a deep-fried catfish platter; a pork chop glazed with Pogue bourbon. An old-school restaurant vibe, a portrait of hometown girl Rosemary Clooney in pride of place, live music on the weekends, and relaxing surroundings—Caproni's checks all the boxes for a memorable evening out.

Caproni's on the River (Courtesy of meetNKY)

## Nearby Alternatives

### Historic Village: Old Washington

Step into Kentucky's frontier past in this village in Maysville with dozens of log cabins dating to the late 1700s, uneven flagstone walkways, and tumble-down cemeteries. Along with antiques, craft shops, and specialty stores are museums, including the **National Underground Railroad Museum**, which houses a documented Safe House.
**Old Main St., Maysville**
**606-563-2596**
visitmaysvilleky.com

### Museum: Rosemary Clooney House

This modest home is steward of the musical legacy of "girl singer" Rosemary Clooney and the largest "White Christmas" collection in the world. See the famous blue frothy "Sisters" dresses and other costumes worn by Clooney and costars in the 1954 holiday film classic, as well as props, movie scripts, letters, photographs, and more.
**106 E Riverside Dr.**
**Augusta, 502-383-9911**
rosemaryclooney.org

### Historic Site: Baker-Bird Winery® & Distillery

Take a guided history tour of America's oldest and largest wine cellar and a distillery that is one of the oldest documented bourbon-distilling sites in the area. Enjoy sips with a cheese plate or picnic pack in the tasting room, tucked within a circa-1850 wine pressing room, or come for brunch or a themed dinner.
**4465 Augusta Chatham Rd.**
**Augusta, 859-620-4965**
bakerbirdwinerydistillery.com

### Restaurant/Lodgings: Beehive Augusta Tavern

The riverfront tavern, originally established in 1796 and now a stop on **the B-Line®**, is home to upscale farm-to-table dining, live music, a bourbon-tasting center, and lots of bourbon. It offers a complete bourbon destination experience with tours of nearby **Augusta Distillery**—home of the "World's Best Bourbon"—and the nine-room **Augusta Guest House**.
**101 W Riverside Dr.**
**Augusta, 606-756-2137**
beehiveaugustatavern.com

## Trip Planning

**Visit Maysville**
**2 E 3rd St., Maysville**
**606-563-2596**
visitmaysvilleky.com
**Augusta/Bracken County Tourism**
**216 Main St., Augusta**
**606-756-2183**
augustaky.com

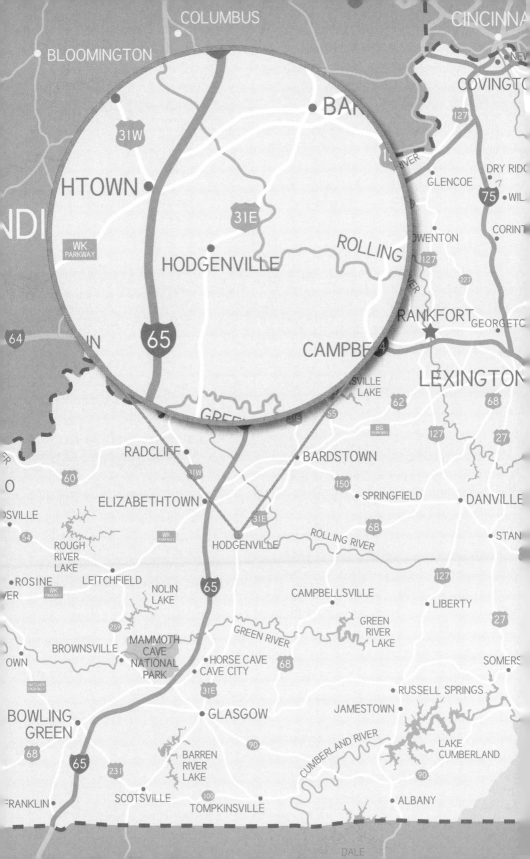

# HODGENVILLE

**A**BRAHAM LINCOLN ONCE called this land a "wild region, with many bears and other wild animals still in the woods." No wild animals these days, but don't be surprised if you see multiple Mary Todds and Abraham Lincolns converging on downtown Hodgenville streets. This is, after all, the Birthplace of Abraham Lincoln—a distinction marked with exuberant celebration every October during Lincoln Days with look-alike contests, parade, rail-splitting competitions, pioneer games, and more.

Sitting along the North Fork of the Nolin River, Hodgenville is a charming small town that is home to two hugely significant national sites: Lincoln's Birthplace and Lincoln's Boyhood Home. Not only that, but a first-class museum, whose art-gallery vignettes give a picture of Lincoln's life and times, sits downtown.

Another landmark attraction is Joel Ray's Lincoln Jamboree, Kentucky's number one family-owned and family-oriented country music and entertainment show since 1954, where Bill Monroe and Whisperin' Bill Anderson once played.

Follow the Downtown Walking Tour to the Old Jail and other sites in Hodgenville's downtown commercial district, on the National Register of Historic Places, and make time to stop at Hinton's Orchard and Farm Market to bite into freshly baked turnovers and play at FarmLand.

# Abraham Lincoln Birthplace National Historic Park

2995 Lincoln Farm Rd. • 270-358-3137 • nps.gov/abli

✓ A humble one-room log cabin. A rough-and-tumble wildland. This is where Abraham Lincoln's story began in 1809 on the Kentucky frontier.

At the Lincoln Birthplace, climb the 56 steps of the Memorial Building, each step representing a year in the life of the 16th president, to see the Symbolic Birth Cabin housed within the columned Beaux Arts–style building. The Lincoln Family Bible, on display at the Birthplace Visitor Center, is among exhibits detailing the Lincolns' time here. Watch the short movie *Abraham Lincoln: The Kentucky Years*. Tour Sinking Spring, an area where young Abraham would have played and fetched water.

See the first home Lincoln remembered at the boyhood home at Knob Creek. He lived here from toddlerhood to age 7 and had memories of sowing pumpkin seeds in a garden his sister planted and listening to his mother read from the Bible.

At the Knob Creek Tavern Visitor Center—opened in 2022 for the first time in 20 years following substantial renovations—see the original headstone of Abraham's baby brother, Thomas.

Abraham Lincoln Birthplace National Historic Park
Memorial Building (Courtesy of NPS Photo)

Lincoln Museum (Courtesy of Pam Spaulding)

# Lincoln Museum

66 Lincoln Sq. · 270-358-3163 · lincolnmuseum-ky.org

✓ This award-winning, accessible museum, a labor of love built by the Hodgenville community, is located only three miles from the Abraham Lincoln Birthplace National Historic Park, in Hodgenville's Downtown Historic District. Housed in side-by-side historic brick buildings, the museum overlooks two Lincoln sculptures, which bookend Lincoln Square: the stately presidential statue and an endearing depiction of the 16th president as a young boy.

Inside the museum are a dozen highly detailed and historically accurate life-size dioramas, authentically staged with period artifacts and wax figures to convey key moments in Lincoln's life—from his early years on the Kentucky frontier to the night of his assassination at Ford's Theatre in Washington, DC.

See these on a self-guided tour, along with rare newspaper clippings; campaign posters; life mask; a gallery of paintings, quilts, and other artwork relating to the Lincoln era; a replica boyhood cabin; and a cabin constructed entirely from pennies—11,368 of them, to be exact.

# Laha's Red Castle

21 Lincoln Sq. · 270-358-9201 · facebook.com/lahasredcastle

✔ Behind every good Laha's Red Castle burger is a great grill. But not just any grill. A vintage 1950s Vulcan Hart grill, built by a manufacturer that traces its history back to 1865 and bought by a company that has been making award-winning burgers since 1934.

Family-owned and operated by four generations of the same family, Laha's secret to success is simple: burgers made the old-fashioned way, with fresh beef on that flavor-enhancing grill. Ryan Jeffries, the great-grandson of founders William and Sally Laha, runs the restaurant today, focusing on old-school customer service and with cooking know-how passed down from one generation to the next.

Besides single and double hamburgers and cheeseburgers, Laha's also serves hot dogs, chili dogs, chili, chicken nuggets, french fries, and onion rings. And speaking in the parlance of old-school burger joints, you can run your patty through the garden with salad dressing, lettuce, tomatoes, and pickles.

Laha's Red Castle (Courtesy of Jessica Wood/Laha's)

## Nearby Alternatives

**Shop:** The Sweet Shoppe & Dessert Cafe

When you see the ginormous red chair by the patio, you've arrived at sweet treat heaven, where more than 30 flavors of fudge—including orange creamsicle, bourbon, and tiger butter—are made fresh daily and have been for more than 20 years. Caramel and gourmet apples, cupcakes, cookies, ice cream treats, and other goodies, too.

**100 S Lincoln Blvd.**
**Hodgenville, 270-358-0424**
facebook.com/
thesweetshoppehodgenville

**Museum:** Swope's Cars of Yesteryear

A 1935 Ford Roadster. A 1923 Packard Sport Touring Car. A 1919 Chandler Motor-Car (the "gangster's car"). Each auto in this classic car collection, ranging from the early 1900s to the 1960s, has a tale to tell. Scan the QR codes for an immersive, self-guided tour at this family-friendly, free-admission museum.

**1080 N Dixie Ave.**
**Elizabethtown, 270-763-6175**
facebook.com/swopemuseum

**Train Museum/Excursions:** Kentucky Railway Museum

Family fun and nostalgia combine aboard a restored passenger train for 22-mile junkets through the Rolling Fork River Valley. Theme cruises include Train Robbery, Christmas Trains, and Dine by Rail. The museum is tucked inside a replica of the original brick L&N New Haven depot. Outside are 100 pieces of rolling stock, including Railway Post Office cars.

**136 S Main St., New Haven**
**800-272-0152**
kyrail.org

**Venue:** Hardin County Playhouse

The little theater that could . . . this hardworking community playhouse has outgrown one space after another as its audience has grown, thanks to first-class productions, including comedies, musicals, and dramas—even original works by local playwrights; a stellar lineup of talent; and the extraordinary devotion of volunteers and patrons.

**600 College Street Rd.**
**Elizabethtown, 270-351-0577**
facebook.com/
hardincountyplayhouse

## Trip Planning:

Visit Hodgenville

**66 Lincoln Sq.**
**270-358-3163**
visithodgenville.com

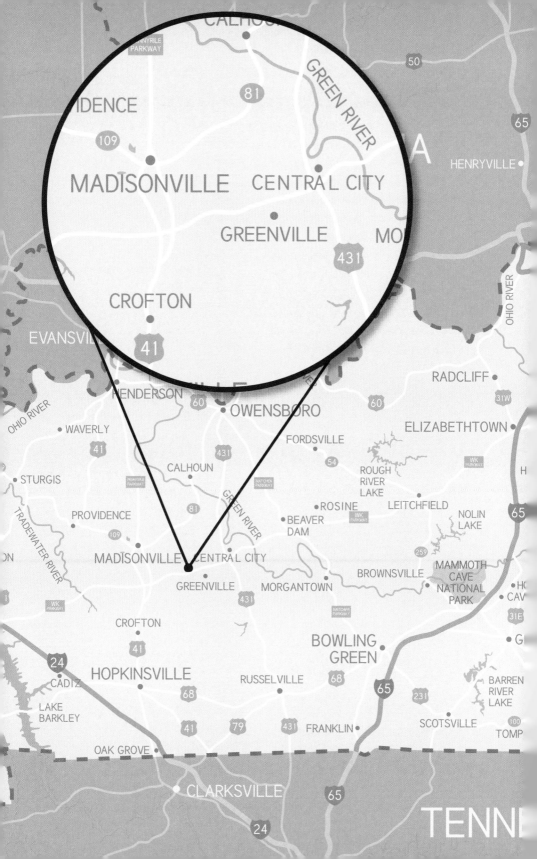

# MUHLENBERG COUNTY

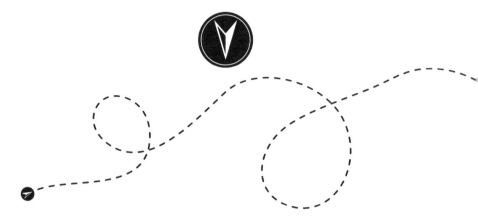

**T**HIS RURAL, ROLLING landscape has had tremendous impact on music's world stage.

It was home to the Everly Brothers, who have influenced generations of musicians and were among the first class of artists inducted into the Rock & Roll Hall of Fame in 1986.

In addition, it was the boyhood home of renowned "thumbpicker" Merle Travis—and consequently is the "Home of Thumbpicking" and site of the annual International Thumbpickers Contest. It is also the place John Prine told the world about in his song "Paradise."

Evidence of these musical prodigies is all over Muhlenberg County—from a memorial to the vocal stylist duo featuring two large guitars and a stone tablet in Central City, to the Merle Travis Music Center in Powderly, to the John Prine Memorial Park in Rochester Dam. Additionally, all three are honored at the Muhlenberg County Music Museum.

The lovely Green River and Lake Malone flow through the county's dreamy landscape. County seat Greenville has a historic town square anchored by a century-old courthouse and crowded with shops. Central City celebrates a rich musical heritage.

# Lake Malone State Park

331 State Rte. 8001, Dunmor • 270-657-2111 • parks.ky.gov

☑ With swimming and sunning on a sandy beach; fishing for bluegill, sunfish, and largemouth bass in a lake gently lapping the shoreline; hiking to geological marvels, including a natural rock bridge; picnicking in shady settings surrounded by trees; and RV and tent camping beneath a sky winking with stars, this state park has "family vacation" written all over it.

The biggest attraction? An outdoor-loving family of 14- and 17-foot benevolent giants called the Big Twigs. Bobber, Oakley, Happy, Annette, Paige, and Watson bring a sense of wonder and enchantment to their lakeside settings and along the park's Laurel Trail—chasing butterflies, roasting marshmallows, catching fireflies, waiting for a fish to bite, and reading a book.

Along with **Laurel Trail**, the two-mile **Twisted Tree** and quarter-mile **Wildflower Trail** show off nature at its most photogenic, with mountain laurel and holly, rock walls and waterfall.

Rounding out amenities at the park are a boat ramp, shelters, and playgrounds; showers, restrooms, and laundry are at the campground.

Lake Malone State Park
(Courtesy of Kentucky
State Parks)

Muhlenberg County Music Museum/Kentucky Motorsports Hall of Fame and Museum (Courtesy of Central City Tourism Commission)

# Muhlenberg County Music Museum

200 N 1st St., Central City • 270-754-5097
facebook.com/CentralCityMusicMuseum

✓ The Everly Brothers' first hit song was recorded more than 65 years ago, in 1957, but people still remember and sing along with the lyrics of "Bye Bye Love."

The story of these hitmaking chart-toppers, who had nearly three dozen Billboard Top 100 singles, is told at this museum located in the city the sibling harmonizers called home. See Everly Brothers records and musical instruments, photographs, awards, and autographed memorabilia, and play one of their songs on the jukebox.

Lyricist extraordinaire John Prine, who immortalized a Muhlenberg County coal town in his song "Paradise," and singer-songwriter Merle Travis are also honored here. Travis, the artist behind "Sixteen Tons," is credited with helping shape rock and roll and country music and is considered one of the most influential guitarists of the 20th century.

Located in a former auto dealership, the museum shares the building with the **Kentucky Motorsports Hall of Fame and Museum**, exhibiting Don Everly's feisty, red 1977 MG among the collection of race cars.

# Stellian's

116 E Broad St., Central City • 270-757-1622 • facebook.com/stellianspizzeria

✓ "Home of the 8LB pizza."

This Italian restaurant throws down a culinary challenge that hungry diners are only too willing to pick up, as in a slice or three of its eight-pound pizza, a double-crust behemoth layered with three-plus-pounds of mozzarella and multiple scoops of a choice of toppings—ground beef, sausage, black olives, banana peppers, pepperoni—then baked, extravagantly sauced, and baked again. And here's the kicker: Stellian's makes 30 to 40 of these beasts daily.

Another culinary claim to fame? Freak Shakes. A riff on the Bloody Mary cocktail-meal, these oh-so-sweet treats are next-level dessert deliciousness. Think strawberry milkshakes swirled with strawberry sauce, encrusted with graham cracker crumbles, topped with a slice of cheesecake, and finished with whipped topping and strawberry slices.

A full bar, dollar bills pinned to the walls, jazz musician mannequins in the windows, and an outgoing staff create a casual, come-on-in atmosphere.

Stellian's (Courtesy of Central City Tourism Commission)

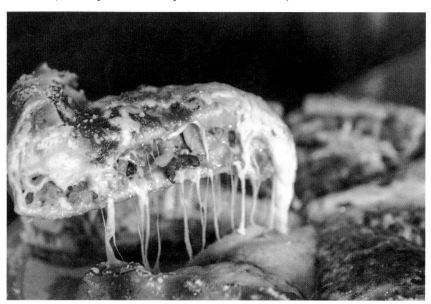

## Nearby Alternatives

### Shopping: The Screen Door

A homespun happy place chock-full of handmade primitives, repurposed items, wooden signs, candles, and more. Look for Kentucky artisan-made furniture, wreaths, floral arrangements, and hand-sewn dolls. It is especially irresistible during fall and holiday seasons, when themed decorations, pictures, and home decor and accessories take over the shop.

30 Big John Dr., Greenville
270-543-9956
facebook.com/thescreendoor

### Outdoors: Mahr Park Arboretum

Among amenities at this 265-acre park are paved walking/biking trails; soft wooded hiking trails; several gardens, including pollinator, butterfly, and native plants; fishing in the ponds or at bordering Lake Pee Wee; kayaking and pedal boating; a nature play area with features made from Douglas fir wood; and a top-ranked championship disc golf course.

55 Mahr Park Dr., Madisonville
270-584-9017
mahrparkarboretum.com

### Outdoors: Dawson Springs

Kentucky's first Certified Trail Town offers the best of both worlds, from the activities of the trail to the delights of the town: hiking **Pennyrile Nature Trail**, biking **Pennyrile State Forest Mountain**, fishing Lake Beshear, and digging into country fried steak at **Ms. Becky's Place** and visiting the **Dawson Springs Museum & Art Center**.

Dawson Springs City Hall
200 W Arcadia Ave., Dawson Springs, 270-797-2781
dawsonspringsky.com

### Bourbon Distillery: The Bard Distillery

The great-great-great-great-grandson of the founder of Bardstown founded this distillery at the school he attended growing up and near farmland established by his great-great-great-grandfather. Co me tour this Art Deco facility being transformed into a world-class distillery, learn about its connections to the coal industry, enjoy a guided tasting, and be welcomed like family.

5080 Hwy. 175 S, Graham
270-338-6543
thebarddistillery.com

## Trip Planning

**Muhlenberg County Tourism Commission**
50 Career Way, Central City
270-641-0276
visitmuhlenberg.com

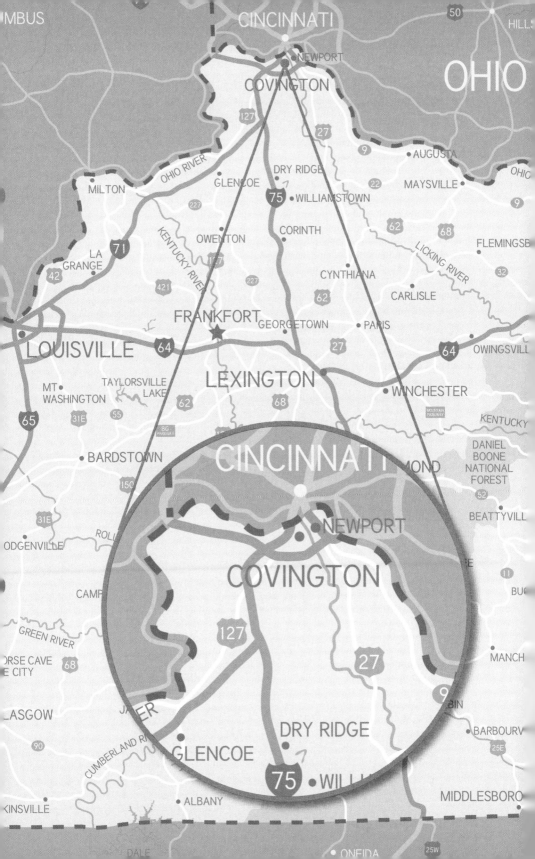

# COVINGTON & NEWPORT

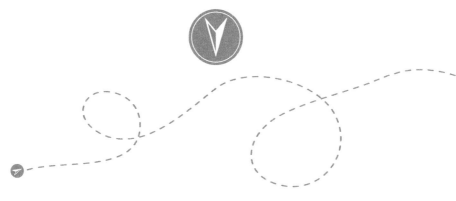

**F**ROM THE BIRTHPLACE of American paleontology at Big Bone Lick Historic Site to the only museum celebrating area history at Behringer-Crawford.

From the first German beer hall and garden modeled after the original in Munich at Hofbräuhaus Newport to the nation's first arboretum within an active recreation park setting at Boone County Arboretum.

From bowmouth guitarfish to bourbon, gangsters to goetta, this community on the banks of the Ohio River has it all. (For the record, goetta is a German-inspired mélange of meat, onions, oats, and spices fried to crispy goodness—an "only here" delicacy annually celebrated during Glier's summertime Goettafest.)

Northern Kentucky has an eye for art, as illustrated by its magnificent Roebling Floodwall Murals, an ear for good music as evidenced by the booked-solid indoor-outdoor concert venue, MegaCorp Pavilion, and a taste for the eclectic as seen on Fairfield Avenue in bustling Bellevue.

It has a spring in its step with live Thoroughbred racing and more at Turfway Park Racing & Gaming, and an oompah-pah in its heart. After all, it is the site of Covington's September Oktoberfest celebration held in shops-and-restaurants mecca, Mainstrasse Village.

# The B-Line

thebline.com

As the Official Gateway to the Kentucky Bourbon Trail®, Northern Kentucky sets the tone for bourbon immersion with the B-Line®. This self-guided bourbon tour whisks aficionadas from river towns to rural settings to sip and sample at bourbon-centric restaurants, bourbon bars, and seven artisan distilleries that are also on the Kentucky Bourbon Trail Craft Tour®.

Find your fortune among the crystal balls at Ludlow's Second Sight Spirits, whose owners display their Las Vegas set-building showmanship in a one-of-a-kind still. Taste handcrafted spirits "made by ghosts" at Boone County Distilling Company.

Unwind over a bourbon craft cocktail before savoring Dutch-inspired cuisine at Lisse Steakhuis, digging into family-recipe fried chicken at a circa-1828 manse at Tousey House Tavern, or munching on an original dish, Goetta Hushpuppies, at Libby's Southern Comfort.

Forget liquid courage. Gain liquid knowledge at Covington's Knowledge Bar & Social Room, creating moody sophistication with its one-of-a-kind lighted art display. Sip signature cocktails next door at Coppin's Restaurant & Bar. Both are part of luxury boutique lodging-dining complex Hotel Covington.

Second Sight Spirits on the B-Line® (Courtesy of meetNKY)

Newport Aquarium (Courtesy of Newport Aquarium)

# Newport Aquarium

One Aquarium Way, Newport • 800-406-3474 • newportaquarium.com

✓ Shimmy along a rope bridge suspended mere inches above a shiver of sharks. Watch a waddle of performing penguins. Gape at a congregation of gators.

What else can you see and do in this million-gallon water world? See a swarm of eels slither about a shipwreck. Follow a balloon-faced pufferfish as it drifts along a 32-foot-long tunnel. Watch a consortium of crabs in Hatchling Harbor, an immersive 25-foot-long Caribbean seagrass habitat where you might also catch sight of "beach builders" (parrotfish) crunching coral into sand.

Spy a herd of seahorses, then style your own at the Seahorse Creation Station. Touch stingrays and sea urchins. Play hide-and-seek in the Frog Bog. Zip down the slide at the Splash & Bubbles Play Climber. Search for the octopus—a master of disguise—in the *Ring of Fire* exhibit.

Located at Newport on the Levee, the aquarium anchors this riverside entertainment complex, home to the open-air Bridgeview Box Park, breweries, restaurants, shops, and galleries.

# Purple Poulet

846 York St., Newport • 859-916-5602 • purplepoulet.com

☑ In the heart of the York Street Historic District, step inside the iconic Green Derby building to a Southern bourbon bistro. It pays homage to Newport's "Sin City" days with a speakeasy party room and piques the palette with dishes inspired by the cuisines of Charleston and New Orleans suffused liberally with the flavors and culture of Kentucky.

With linens on the tables inside and umbrella tables on the bricked patio outside, original textured metal on the ceiling and art on the walls (including paintings of variously colored poulets or chickens) plus 500 (and counting) bourbons at the bar, this stop on **the B-Line** is an ideal setting for special occasions or any evening out when the goal is a fun gathering with farm-fresh food and fine Kentucky bourbon.

Signature dishes include rave-review fried chicken served with black pepper gravy, shrimp and grits with bourbon-cream pan gravy, and the chef's twist on the Kentucky Hot Brown.

Purple Poulet (Courtesy of meetNKY)

## Nearby Alternatives

**Historic Tour:** American Legacy Tours' Newport Gangster Tour

Meet a few dirty, double-crossing rats from "Sin City's" gambling and bootlegging past—the Vegas before Vegas, when mobs ruled, and their molls played cool. This hugely popular guided tour begins at Gangsters Dueling Piano Bar, a former casino, and crisscrosses some of 1930s Newport's most notorious streets.

**18 E 5th St., Newport**
**859-951-8560**
americanlegacytours.com

**Museum:** Vent Haven Museum

Is it creepy to have 1,100 pairs of eyes openly gaping at you? See for yourself at the world's only museum dedicated to ventriloquism: six galleries of dummies and puppets; permanent exhibits on Edgar Bergen, Shari Lewis, Darci Lynne, Jeff Dunham, and others; interactive activities; and a chance to practice your vent skills.

**33 W Maple Ave., Fort Mitchell**
**859-341-0461**
venthaven.org

**Historic Site:** Rabbit Hash/ Rabbit Hash General Store

Go ahead: scratch the mayor's belly. One of the few US towns with a canine mayor, tiny Rabbit Hash is pure Americana. Poke about the circa-1830s general store for artisan-made brooms and pottery. Book an overnight at the Old Hashienda. Spend a yesteryear kind of day, taking in a barn dance and idling along the riverbank.

**10021 Lower River Rd.**
**Rabbit Hash, 859-586-7744**
rabbithash.com

**River Excursion/Restaurant:** BB Riverboats

Glide along the Ohio River aboard a Victorian beauty—the *Belle of Cincinnati*, flagship of this paddle wheeler fleet recalling those Mark Twain days of the riverboat era. A variety of sightseeing, brunch, lunch, dinner, and themed cruises are offered: murder mystery, moonlight, music, and more—stunning views on the side. And at Halloween, the *USS Nightmare* brings the scares with haunted tours.

**101 Riverboat Row, Newport**
**800-261-8586**
bbriverboats.com

## Trip Planning

MeetNKY | Northern Kentucky Convention & Visitors Bureau

**50 E RiverCenter Blvd., Ste. 1100, Covington, 859-261-4677**
meetnky.com

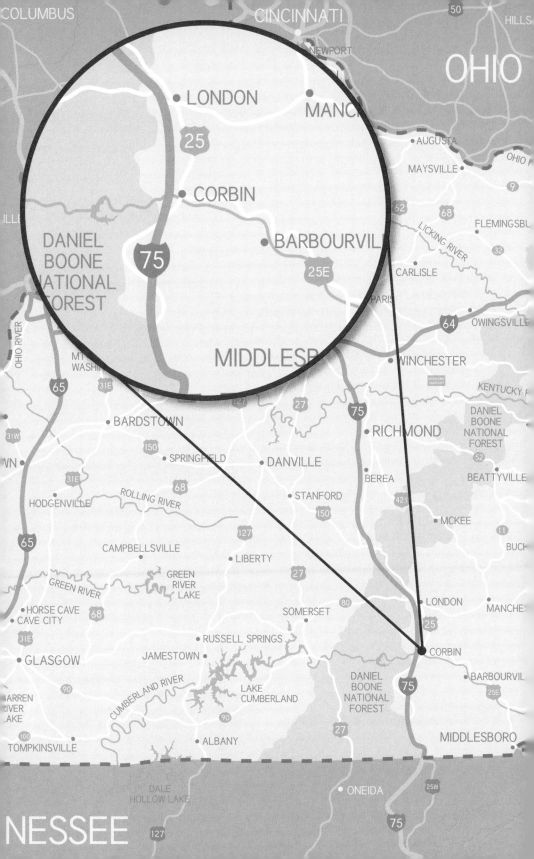

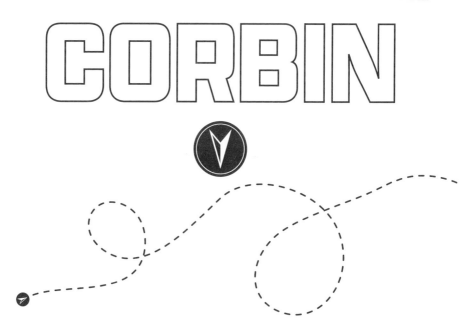

# CORBIN

**C**LAIMING THE LARGEST waterfall in Kentucky—a cascading curtain stretching 125 feet wide and plummeting more than 60 feet into a gorge—as well as colossal cookware, a fiercely guarded secret recipe, acres of forest, miles of wooded trails, and a lake so irrepressibly picturesque it seems enchanted, Corbin is the outdoor adventurer's paradise found.

It is also a place of discovery, where visitors can indulge in a burgeoning downtown restaurant scene. Bite into a Big Ass Pretzel at the Wrigley Taproom or sip one of 60-plus Kentucky bourbons. Hear up-and-comers on the country music scene along with national touring acts while munching on a pile of Tangled Up Tumbleweeds (onion rings) at Austin City Saloon.

Go old-school and play dozens of pinball machines at the Pinball Museum of Corbin. Find some (but not all) of the herbs and spices that make Kentucky Fried Chicken so finger lickin' good in the Sanders Park Secret Recipe Garden, and cross a 1902 L&N Railroad bridge to a charming city park.

Get back to nature, hiking the Laurel River Lake and Laurel Bridge trails for views of caves, shoreline, and rock formations. Follow Sheltowee Trace Trail from the KY 192 Trailhead to Laurel Dam and enjoy white sandy beaches.

# Cumberland Falls State Resort Park

7351 Hwy. 90 • 606-528-4121
parks.ky.gov

✓ Magnificent Cumberland Falls is one of the few places in the world to experience that rarest of phenomena, the moonbow. With its ghostly white arc, this white or lunar rainbow entrances visitors to the "Niagara of the South" who are lucky enough to witness the moonbow's appearance, which happens less than 10 percent as often as a regular rainbow. (Moonbow dates are found on the park's website.)

Located within Daniel Boone National Forest, Cumberland Falls crashes down a 68-foot sandstone cliff, creating the perfect amount of mist so that when it is struck by enough moonlight, a moonbow emerges. The best place to view the falls in all its thundering splendor? Eagle Falls Trail—where this trail's namesake waterfall plunges 44 feet into the Cumberland River.

Climb the Pinnacle Knob 1937 Fire Tower. Gallop through the forest on horseback. Mine for rubies, emeralds, and other gemstones. Cozy up to the massive stone fireplace in historic **DuPont Lodge** and drink in the surrounding scenery while dining at **Riverview Restaurant**.

Cumberland Falls State Resort Park (Courtesy of Kentucky State Parks)

Laurel River Lake (Courtesy of Ben Childers/Corbin KY Tourism)

# World Chicken Festival

140 Faith Assembly Church Rd.. London • 606-878-6900 • chickenfestival.com

✓ Have a white suit, black spectacles, and a bucket o' chicken handy? You could be a contestant in the Colonel Sanders Look-A-Like Contest during the World Chicken Festival, held every September only 14 miles from where the original Colonel Sanders invented Kentucky Fried Chicken—the Bluegrass State's culinary gift to the world.

The contest is part of the four-day celebration that also features fried chicken cooked to crispy golden deliciousness in the World's Largest Stainless-Steel Skillet—an 11-gauge, hot-rolled stainless-steel frying pan measuring 10 feet, six inches in diameter and eight inches deep, sporting an eight-foot handle, and weighing a whopping 700 pounds. The skillet, which requires 300 gallons of cooking oil, can fry 600 quarters of chicken . . . at one time!

Other activities include a chicken cook-off, a "chicken invasion" featuring flocks of painted wooden chickens, Grand Parade, Chicken "Trickin" Trivia Contest, and the Chicken Wattle Whiskers and Beard Contest, plus arts, crafts, food, and music.

# Sanders Cafe and Museum

688 US Hwy. 25 W • 606-528-2163 • sanderscafe.com

☑ In 1940, Colonel Harland Sanders blended 11 hand-selected herbs and spices, forever changing the global culinary landscape and giving hungry diners permission to lick their fingers. Calling it "Sunday Dinner, Seven Days a Week," Sanders served his Original Recipe fried chicken at Sanders Court and Cafe in Corbin—the Birthplace of Kentucky Fried Chicken.

Diners today can order a bucket of chicken at the place where it all began. Now the Sanders Cafe and Museum, this National Register of Historic Places site features Sanders's 1940s model motel room created to win over "the lady of the house" with its show of squeaky-clean space.

See this and other artifacts, including the kitchen where Sanders developed his secret KFC® formula, vintage advertising, hand-painted menu boards, and other memorabilia. And that life-size Colonel Sanders, decked out in his legendary white suit and relaxing on a bench? It's the perfect photo-op stop.

Sanders Cafe and Museum (Courtesy of Kentucky Tourism)

## Nearby Alternatives

### Accommodations/Outdoors: Sheltowee Trace Adventure Resort

Feel the spray, hear the roar, and ratchet up the thrills with guided rainbow and moonbow mist river adventures to Cumberland Falls. White-water rafting, unguided duckie trips, tubing, canoeing, kayaking, hiking, biking, zip lining, and so. Much. More. At night, bunk down in a covered wagon, cozy cabin, or **Star Falls Resort** cabin.

2001 Hwy. 90
606-526-RAFT
ky-rafting.com

### Outdoors: Laurel River Lake

Mother Nature giddily shows off at this lake, so picture-postcard pretty with sparkling clean water, undulating forested shoreline, hushed coves, and craggy cliff tops that it seems the stuff of make-believe. But it's real—and with scuba diving, fishing, boating, camping, skiing, and wildlife viewing, it's a nature lover's happy place.

**Daniel Boone National Forest London Ranger District**
fs.usda.gov

### Outdoors: Levi Jackson Wilderness Road Park

Swing, zip, walk, wobble, crawl. Daredevils head straight for the treetops for an aerial adventure that throws down the challenge with five sky-high trails with 60 elements including zip lines, suspended tunnels, rope bridges. It's all about safe family fun and making memories, with camping, swimming, mini golf, and hiking, plus the **Mountain Life Museum & Gift Shop**.

998 Levi Jackson Mill Rd.
London
606-330-2130
levijacksonpark.com

### Outdoors: Kentucky Wildlands Waterfall Trail

Follow the trail through a land of more than 800 waterfalls to 17 superlative cascades, from Seventy Six Falls, a sight to behold as it plunges downward nearly 90 feet, to the Big One—Cumberland Falls—from a curtain of water named after Cherokee Princess Cornblossom to Dog Slaughter Falls with irresistible blue plunge pool.

**Eastern and Southern Kentucky**
explorekywildlands.com
**Click on "The Kentucky Wildlands"/"Our Trails"**

## Trip Planning

### Corbin Tourism and Convention Commission

101 N Depot St.
606-528-8860
corbinkytourism.com

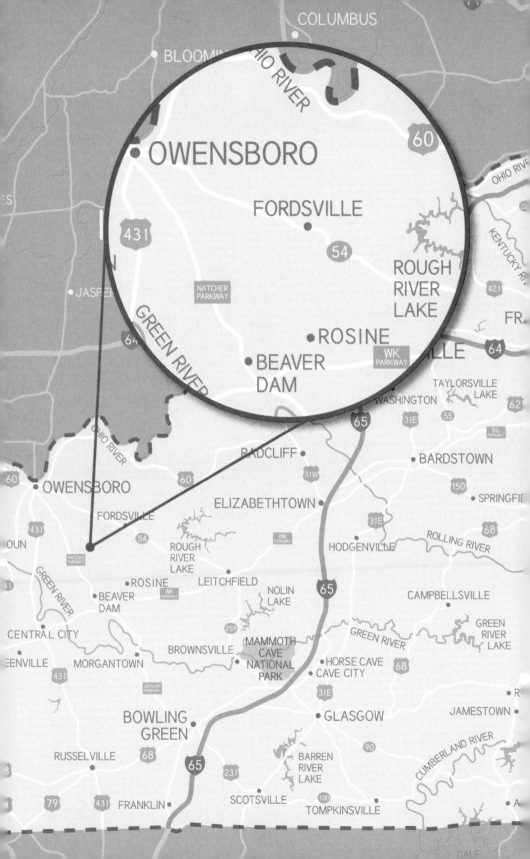

# OWENSBORO & ROSINE

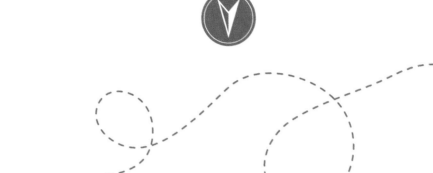

**K**ENTUCKY'S FOURTH-LARGEST CITY of Owensboro is known as the Bluegrass Capital of the World, the Bar-B-Q Capital of the World (sorry, Kansas City), and, more specifically, the Barbecued Mutton Capital of the World.

Bluegrass and barbecue . . . two signature Kentucky items that pair beautifully together. Two more? Bourbon and Broadway. As the cultural hub of western Kentucky, Owensboro is home to a stellar lineup of arts organizations, including the Owensboro Symphony Orchestra and Broadway in Owensboro. It has also been in the business of bourbon for a long time, with a distilling location dating back to 1885.

Other claims to fame? Hugging a bend along the Ohio River, Owensboro is privy to gorgeous river views. Western Kentucky Botanical Garden is a lushly designed masterpiece, with a nationally recognized Daylily Garden Display and June Dazzling Daylily Festival. The largest known sassafras tree in the world—a photo-op-stop worthy 21 feet in circumference—has its roots here. Smothers Park on the riverfront, the "Top Playground in the World," wows kids of all ages.

# Bluegrass Music Hall of Fame & Museum

311 W 2nd St., Owensboro
270-926-7891 • bluegrasshall.org

☑ Uncle Pen's fiddle. Pete Seeger's banjo. Josh Graves's guitar. See these musical instruments and others, plus memorabilia relating to the pioneers and innovators of bluegrass music, at the only cultural center in the world dedicated exclusively to this genre born in Kentucky.

Located on Owensboro's riverfront, the center brings to life the story of bluegrass through the people, performers, instruments, artifacts, and the music itself that influenced and shaped this uniquely American sound, one that continues to evolve and claims fans in every part of the world.

Take the audio guided tour and drift on down the River of Sound to learn about the legends, from Bill Monroe to contemporary artists. Sit in on live jams, held Saturday and Sunday afternoons. Come for live music events staged at the museum, indoors and out. Bring your own instrument to the **ROMP Festival**, produced by the center and held annually in June, with artist-led instrument workshops, jams, and music.

Bluegrass Music Hall of Fame & Museum (Courtesy of Kentucky Tourism)

Bill Monroe Homeplace (Courtesy of Kentucky Tourism)

# Bill Monroe Homeplace

6210 US-62 E, Beaver Dam • 270-363-9501 • ohiocounty.com/billmonroe

Sitting on Jerusalem Ridge in Beaver Dam is the Bill Monroe Homeplace, the boyhood home the Father of Bluegrass referenced in his song, "I'm on My Way Back to the Old Home." The trim white clapboard home holds family photographs, furnishings, and memorabilia.

Bluegrass music fans from around the world make a pilgrimage to Rosine and sites connected to the legend, including Rosine Cemetery. Here, Monroe's final resting place is marked by an impressive obelisk-style monument.

Nearby, the **Rosine Barn Jamboree** houses the stage on which Monroe himself once performed. This National Register of Historic Places site hosts bluegrass, gospel, and country music Friday nights, March through early December, as well as impromptu jams.

Pay a call at **Uncle Pen's Cabin**, home of one of Monroe's greatest musical influences, his beloved uncle, fiddle player Pendleton Vandiver. See a treasure trove of instruments, performance clothes, cowboy hats and boots, photographs—even Monroe's Cadillac DeVille—at the **Bill Monroe Museum**.

# Moonlite Bar-B-Q Inn

2840 W Parrish Ave., Owensboro • 270-684-8143 • moonlite.com

☑ It would be culinary criminality to visit the Bar-B-Q Capital of the World and not taste the barbecue—especially when this restaurant, an Owensboro tradition for 60-plus years, does barbecue so exquisitely. So do what the locals do and dig into two original Kentucky dishes: burgoo, a slow-cooked, well-seasoned stew of mutton, beef or other meat and variety of veggies, and mutton barbecue and sop—Kentucky for sauce.

The restaurant serves an impressive buffet: a variety of meats, comfort-food sides like mac 'n' cheese, seasoned green beans, cinnamon apple slices, and baked beans.

Additionally, hearty dinners are served, starring a choice of barbecue (chicken, mutton, pork, and beef) and accompanied by toasted bun or corn-bread muffins and a choice of two sides—potato salad, beans, slaw, cottage cheese, fries, tossed salad. If, heaven forbid, you pass on the barbecue, there are also catfish and shrimp dinners.

**TIP:** Moonlite Bar-B-Q Inn is a stop on the **Western Kentucky Barbecue Trail**, featuring over 15 restaurants, each offering its own signature barbecue.

Moonlite Bar-B-Q Inn (Courtesy of Kentucky Tourism)

## Nearby Alternatives

### Museum: Owensboro Museum of Fine Art

This free-admission house museum and art gallery showcases traveling exhibitions and rotating shows from a permanent collection of American, European, and Asian fine and decorative arts dating from the 15th century to the present, including late 19th-/early 20th-century German stained glass windows. The **Holiday Forest Festival of Trees** is held here, among other festivals.

**901 Frederica St., Owensboro**
**270-685-3181**
omfa.us

### Bourbon Distillery: Green River Distilling Company

Sip bourbon. Thieve bourbon from the barrel. Walk bourbon's hallowed grounds. Here is one of the world's oldest bourbon distilleries in a town with a bourbon-making heritage dating back to the 1800s—once home to 20 distilleries. Go behind the scenes and back in time to the only Kentucky distillery closed by Prohibition that reopened on the same spot.

**10 Distillery Rd., Owensboro**
**270-691-9001**
greenriverwhiskey.com

### Shopping/Restaurant: Preservation Station

Thirty-nine thousand square feet, 60-plus shops, special Market Days . . . you actually could drop from shopping this sprawling former elementary school packed with antiques, uniques, and boutique treasures—chicken coops to collectibles. Thankfully, shoppers can revive at the restaurant, open for lunch and Sunday buffet, with a Southern-style menu—wine and beer, too.

**9661 Hwy. 56, Owensboro**
**270-616-7007**
visitpreservationstation.com

### Museum: Owensboro Museum of Science and History

Crawl through tubes, over bridges, and under a choo-choo train. Put on a puppet show. Grab a hard hat and head underground and into the 1930s at Rudy Mine to experience a day in the life of a miner. Dive into hands-on fun from the PlayZeum's indoor playground to the SpeedZeum, chock-full of racing cars.

**122 E 2nd St., Owensboro**
**270-687-2732**
owensboromuseum.org

## Trip Planning

**Visit Owensboro**
**215 E 2nd St., 270-926-1100**
visitowensboro.com

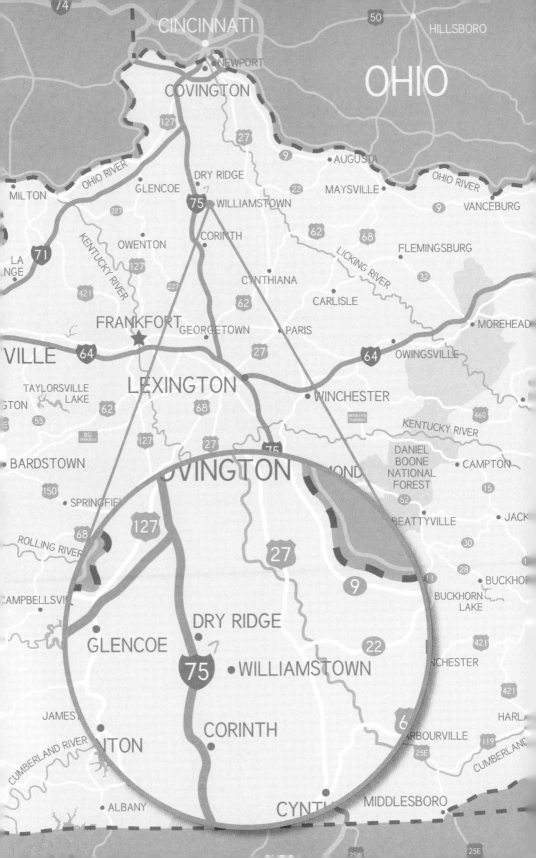

# WILLIAMSTOWN

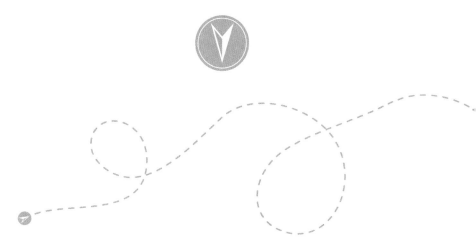

**S**MALL-TOWN VIBE, BIG outdoor vacationland. Williamstown combines the best of both worlds, from little treasures to supersized entertainment. Join the locals at Belle's BBQ, a watering hole that welcomes with live music, ladies nights, and cookie-making classes. Pint-size fishers can drop a line for largemouth bass at local fishing hole Bullock Pen Lake. Hometown theater courtesy of Stage Right Musical Theatre Company charms the audience with professional-quality productions.

On the other end of the size spectrum, the Ark Encounter wows with zip lines and aerial course, fossil hunt, children's playground, carousel ride, and Ararat Ridge Zoo with petting area, animal shows, and camel rides—not to mention the showstopper main attraction, the colossal ark.

Shopping options include antique havens like the Mercantile with 50 vendors and Uptown Vintage with an array of primitives plus BathBar Soap with its handmade scented treasures and the Quilt Shop and its array of beautiful fabrics.

From hiking haven J. B. Miller Park with its 10-acre lake, to free-admission Williamstown Splash Park arrayed with benches and picnic tables, to scenic boating and swimming lake, to downtown shops made for souvenir browsing and buying, Williamstown has all the makings of a fun, old-fashioned family vacation.

# Ark Encounter

1 Ark Encounter Dr. · 855-284-3275 · arkencounter.com

☑ "The animals went in two by two/The elephant and the kangaroo...." If you've ever wondered exactly how cavernous Noah's Ark had to be to house all of creation's animals for 40 days and nights of flooding, the Ark Encounter will blow you away with the numbers. Based on biblical blueprints, which used cubits for measuring (the length from elbow to the tip of the longest finger), the ark stands 51 feet high, 510 feet long, and 85 feet wide.

And that is exactly what you'll see dry-docked in Williamstown, rising from the rolling landscape and offering three decks packed with state-of-the-art exhibits, including Noah's living quarters. The full-scale, family-friendly theme park also has a "time machine" virtual reality experience, hands-on educational programming, and the two-story Emzara's Kitchen buffet-style restaurant with views of the Ark.

TIP: Pair Ark Encounter with sister attraction, the Creation Museum in Petersburg, featuring animatronics, planetarium, botanical gardens, and gorgeous ChristmasTown holiday event.

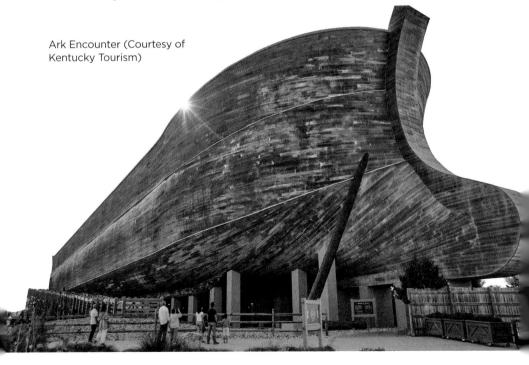

Ark Encounter (Courtesy of Kentucky Tourism)

Williamstown Lake (Courtesy of Grant County Tourist & Convention Commission)

# Williamstown Lake/Williamstown Marina

290 Boot Dock Rd. · 859-823-0645 · wtownmarina.com

✔ Northern Kentucky's largest lake is the setting for an idyllic family camping getaway. Rent a camper or pitch a tent on a swath of green and toast marshmallows at the fireplace. Swim and splash about, launch a canoe or kayak, or grab your stand-up paddleboard and glide across the calm waters of this 330-acre recreational lake.

Picnic and play along more than 25 miles of tree-lined shoreline. Fish for bluegill, green sunfish, or redhorse sucker. Spend a lazy, summer camp kind of weekend at a lakefront vacation home with all the amenities.

Rent a pontoon from Williamstown Marina for a day of waterplay. Grab dinner at the seasonal Dockside Pizza and Pub and join fellow campers and visitors for a warm-weather Friday or Saturday night filled with entertainment—live music, luaus, and fireworks.

If a visit to Williamstown Lake feels like time spent playing hooky from real life, it's only because Williamstown Lake was created exactly for this purpose.

# Kellie's Homestead Restaurant/Barnwood Bravo Theater | 1108 Fashion Ridge Rd., Dry Ridge · 859-903-9477
kellieshomestead.com

✓ An all-in-one, full-on entertainment outing with food, sweet treats, toy train, artisan-made souvenirs, and a stage filled with music and magic—all in a country setting. The family-owned Kellie's Homestead is an afternoon or evening packed with the kind of fun of which memories are made.

Dining is pure Southern comfort—fried chicken, classic meat loaf, and turkey smothered in homemade gravy at the restaurant, or opt for dinner and a show, featuring buffet favorites like beef tips, buttered noodles, and creamy, cheesy pasta bake. Dig in while watching a magician perform tricks, a tribute band honor Elvis or the queens of country music, or a dynamic duo perform jukebox hits. No matter the entertainment theme, rest assured it is rated fantastic for family friendly.

Poke about Barnwood Gifts and Art for handmade items: wooden toys, afghans, pillows, decorated T-shirts, pottery, soaps, key chains, and other goodies.

Kellie's Homestead Restaurant and Barnwood
Bravo Theater (Courtesy of Kellie's Homestead)

## Nearby Alternatives

**Outdoors/Museum:** General Butler State Resort Park
Explore the 1859 Greek Revival–style Butler-Turpin Home Museum. Catch the setting sun from the overlook as it melts into the Ohio River. Sit down to country cooking in Twin Rivers Restaurant. Hike, pedal boat, play miniature golf, join the naturalist for a program, or fish. No fishing pole? No problem. The park will lend you one for free.
**1608 Hwy. 227, Carrollton**
**502-732-4384, parks.ky.gov**

**Winery:** Brianza Gardens and Winery
Beautiful grounds and showy gardens inspired by the wineries of Northern Italy complement the award-winning wine and live music entertainment (weekends) at this gorgeous winery set in the countryside. Enjoy a wine flight or picnic package or book a romantic getaway at one of its three lodgings set amid the exquisite scenery.
**14611 Salem Creek Rd.**
**Crittenden**
**859-445-9369 (Tasting Room)**
**brianzagardens.com**

**Outdoors:** Elk Creek Hunt Club
Golf with a shotgun? Experience the thrill of wing shooting at this world-class sporting clay resort for all experience levels. Elk Creek has three different courses spread over 1,200 acres, each consisting of 12 to 16 stations with two to three traps per station. Bonus: Elk Creek Vineyards is two minutes down the road. This is destination dining and wining, plus live music on Fridays and Saturdays.
**1860 Georgetown Rd.**
**Owenton, 502-484-4569**
**elkcreekhuntclub.com**

**Outdoors:** Kincaid Lake State Park
Peaceful and quiet in a beautiful woodland setting, this state park is perfect for family camping trips with lots of options for recreation: rent a kayak or pedal boat, drop a line in the lake, hike the Spicebush and Ironwood Trails, swim at the park's pool, play tennis and nine-hole miniature golf, or spread a picnic by the playground.
**565 Kincaid Park Rd., Falmouth**
**859-654-3531**
**parks.ky.gov**

## Trip Planning

Grant County Tourist & Convention Commission
**1350 N Main St.**
**800-382-7117**
**visitgrantky.com**

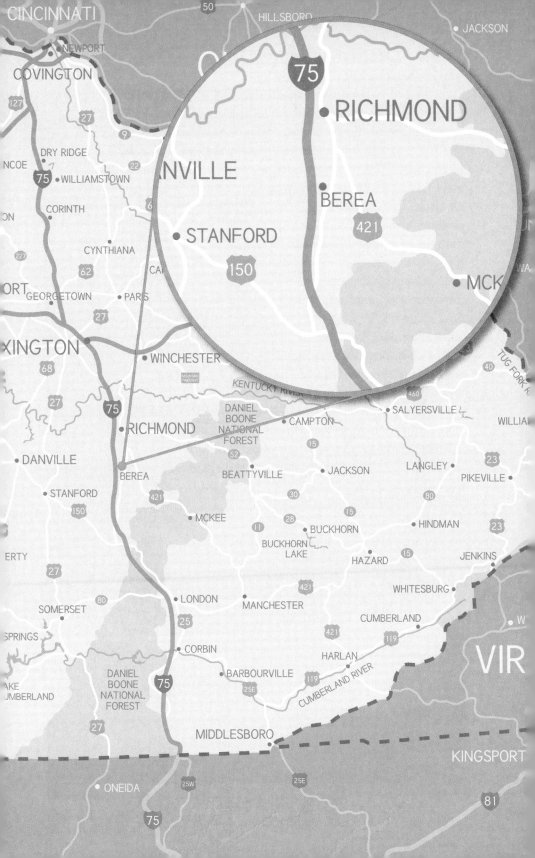

# BEREA

**A**RTISTIC, HISTORIC, IDYLLIC. The Folk Arts and Crafts Capital of Kentucky is a thriving community of artists, dreamers, and doers set in the Appalachian foothills.

From the student crafts showcases of College Square to working artist studios, Civil War sites, and architectural and historical tours in the Artisan Village to the arts-and-antiques enclave of Chestnut Street and the arts mecca that is the Kentucky Artisan Center, Berea is steeped in a handcrafting culture and a spirit of independence.

It is home to Berea College, dating back to 1855, which began as a one-room schoolhouse set amid the wilderness and is consistently named among the top regional colleges in the South. The history of the town is intrinsically tied to the college, whose unique work program involves students in every aspect of community.

It is a place for uncomplicated and romantic escapes: a moonlit kayak glide on picturesque Owsley Fork Lake with picnic basket supper, a bluegrass music concert on the grounds of Old Town Artisan Village, and a tree-house getaway with Homegrown Hideaways to stargaze and reconnect with nature and self.

# Kentucky Artisan Center/ Artisan Village/LearnShops

200 Artisan Way • 859-985-5448 • kentuckyartisancenter.ky.gov

✔ Arrive early; there is a lot to take in, and a lot you may wish to take home. The Kentucky Artisan Center has tantalizing displays of works from over 850 Kentucky artists—each an expression of the state's folk traditions and handcrafting heritage: decorative pottery pieces, glassworks, furniture, quilts, jewelry, paintings, sculptures for the garden.

In the Artisan Village, follow the "Studio Artists at Berea: Artists at Work" icons to watch makers work through the stages of creation, from inspiration through completion: forming clay into one-of-a-kind Santa figures, transforming sterling silver and other metals into jewelry, and shaping 2,000-degree glass into sea creatures.

Coax your inner artist out during a workshop in making journals, corn-husk dolls, brooms, clay art, or other handicrafts during the Festival of LearnShops, held annually in July and during the holiday-themed Make It, Take It, Give It LearnShops in November and December.

Berea LearnShops (Courtesy of Berea Tourism)

The Pinnacles at Berea College's Indian Fort (Courtesy of Berea Tourism)

# The Pinnacles at Berea College's Indian Fort

2047 Big Hill Rd. • 859-756-3315
Berea College Forestry Outreach Center • visitberea.com

✔ Drop. Dead. Gorgeous. In a combination of hues and textures any painter would be proud to mix on a palette, spectacular views await at the top of the Pinnacles' half dozen trails, including East and West Pinnacle, Devil's Kitchen, and Indian Fort Lookout. See layers of Appalachian Mountain peaks, sometimes shrouded in fog, the variegated greens of the forest saturating the valleys, blue sky stretching on. And on. And on. Come autumn, Mother Nature takes it all up a notch with a rich tapestry of blazing color.

Because of the views, as well as the proximity to Daniel Boone National Forest and accessibility to the shops, sights, and delights of Berea, the Pinnacles, located in the Berea College Forest, are among Kentucky's best and most scenic hikes. The trail system is part of Berea College's Indian Fort and its 9,000 forested acres, which is also part of Kentucky's Wilderness Road Heritage Highway, unspooling from the Cumberland Gap to Berea.

# Honeysuckle Dining and Bourbon House

100 Churchill Ct. • 859-625-2438
churchills.co/honeysuckle

✓ Dine inside the former Churchill Weavers building where luxury sofa throws and baby blankets were handwoven from 1922 to 2007. Today, seasonally changing menus with locally sourced ingredients present a mix of regional classics spiced up with world influences.

Signature appetizers include hand-cut truffle fries seasoned with shredded parmesan, truffle oil, and house herbs and deep-fried frog legs served with a house-made spicy maple glaze. Among entrées, fan favorites are the coffee-crusted Berkshire pork chop with collard greens and goat cheese mashed potatoes, and the pan-seared ocean trout, zested up with onion, zucchini, mushroom, and chowchow—a tangy vegetable relish starring summer's vegetable bounty.

Honeysuckle's desserts are headlined by the Ale-8 Apple Dumpling, starring Kentucky's original, secret-recipe soft drink, Ale-8-One, made in nearby Winchester since 1926. The bar stocks over 100 bourbons and has a selection of Kentucky craft beers on draft. Also here: bourbon flights, live music on Thursday nights, and cocktail classes by request.

Honeysuckle Dining and
Bourbon House
(Courtesy of
Mary Ann West)

## Nearby Alternatives

**Restaurant/Inn: Historic Boone Tavern Hotel & Restaurant**

Owned by Berea College, the hotel and restaurant are staffed in part by students. Sleep in a guest room cozied up with handcrafted furniture. Sample the spoon bread appetizer or dine on signature delectable, Chicken Flakes in a Bird's Nest. Borrow a complimentary bicycle and pedal to nearby shops and artist galleries, or zip around town by electric bike.

**100 S Main St. North
800-366-9358**
boonetavernhotel.com

**Outdoors: Stepping Stone Ranch at Deer Run Stable**

Pull on your riding boots and explore this hundred-acre wood on guided scenic trail rides through Daniel Boone Country. Trot into hardwood forests, splashing through creeks, passing a pre–Civil War cemetery and 1700s-era cabins, and spotting wildflowers and wildlife along the way. All levels of experience are welcome.

**2001 River Circle Dr., Richmond
615-268-9960**
steppingstoneranchco.com

**Outdoors/Historic Site: Fort Boonesborough State Park**

A reconstructed working fort with blockhouses, cabins, and furnishings narrate the story of Kentucky's second settlement (Harrodsburg was first in 1774), which Daniel Boone hacked from the wilderness in 1775. Living historians present 18th-century life skills and period craft demonstrations. Enjoy camping, hiking, boating to the geologically ancient Kentucky Palisades, and shopping for handmade pioneer items.

**4375 Boonesboro Rd.
Richmond, 859-527-3131**
parks.ky.gov

**Outdoors: Snug Hollow Farm Bed-and-Breakfast**

Wander among wildflowers and along creeks. Meditate through a meadowland labyrinth. Dine on freshly prepared garden-to-table cuisine and let nature's soundtrack lull you to sleep in a handcrafted cabin that is pure country charm. Nearby, paddle Lake Reba or buy a Spoon Bread Baker at Tater Knob Pottery, which highlights Appalachian artworks.

**790 Cr-1221 #8951, Irvine
606-723-4786**
snughollow.com

## Trip Planning

**Berea Tourism Commission**
**3 Artist Cir., 859-986-2540**
visitberea.com

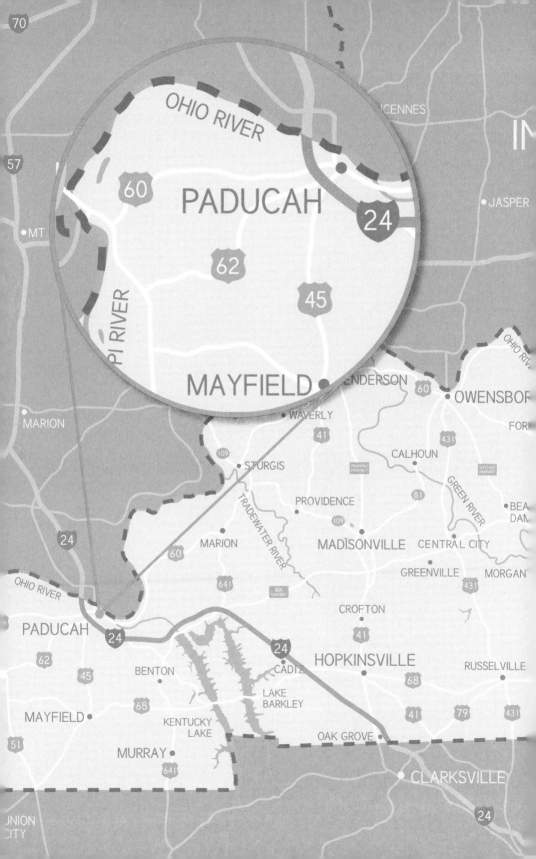

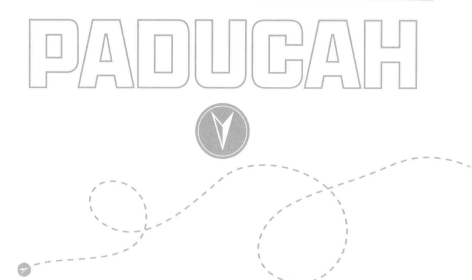

# PADUCAH

**W**ITH A RICH, spirited, and diverse cultural arts landscape offering everything from live theater to exhibitions to classical symphonic performances, it is easy to see why this City of Crafts & Folk Art earned the designation of UNESCO Creative City. Paducah is one of less than 10 such cities in the United States so recognized by the United Nations Educational, Scientific & Cultural Organization and among less than 300 worldwide.

A sophisticated river town set at the confluence of the Ohio and Tennessee Rivers, Paducah has a beautiful, historic, and walkable downtown, and overflows with cultural assets: Carson Center for the Performing Arts, Clemens Fine Art Center, Maiden Alley Cinema and Gallery, Market House Theatre, Paducah Symphony Orchestra, Yeiser Art Center. Savor local tastes amidst architecturally beautiful surroundings in Paducah's Historic District, dining on perfectly seasoned steaks at Dot's Eat Place, recognized by the James Beard Foundation as an American Classic, and Pipers Tea and Coffee House, especially beguiling during the holidays when the shop presents its "12 Days of Pipers Hot Chocolate."

Paducah reignited an entire neighborhood through its award-winning Artist Relocation Program and today working artists, students, and artists-in-residence create and show their work in the 26-square-block Lower Town Arts District, now home to the Paducah School of Art & Design.

# National Quilt Museum

215 Jefferson St. • 270-442-8856 • quiltmuseum.org

☑ At the heart of Paducah's dynamic arts and entertainment scene is the National Quilt Museum, housing a collection of over 600 extraordinary quilts from America and around the world in celebration of the contemporary quilt experience.

Find exhibitions featuring a variety of techniques and themes, such as large-scale designs, antique and vintage quilts, and issues affecting Black women in America as expressed through these soft treasures. Take part in a workshop. Explore quilt-making's diversity of color, style, and subject range. Visit in April for Paducah's AQS QuiltWeek event.

Paducah has several quilt and fabric shops, each offering a unique experience, from hand-selected cotton quilting fabric and hand-dyed fabrics to workshops in English paper piecing and other fiber crafts to an art collection of quilts and a Museum Shop & Book Store. Located at the National Quilt Museum, it features Kentucky crafted items and hundreds of quilting and quilt-related books.

There's a reason Paducah is nicknamed Quilt City USA.

National Quilt Museum
(Courtesy of Paducah
Convention & Visitors Bureau)

Wall to Wall floodwall murals (Courtesy of Paducah Convention & Visitors Bureau)

# Wall to Wall Floodwall Murals

100 Water St. • 270-519-1321
paducahwalltowall.com

✔ Paducah's most popular 24/7 art history attraction is also one of Kentucky's most visited attractions. With Paducah's floodwall as its canvas, Wall to Wall unspools "Portraits of Paducah's Past" over a three-block stretch along Water Street.

Native American Mound Builders, frontier life, the Lewis and Clark Expedition, 1940s Main Street, the pivotal role railroads played in Paducah, Paducah's African American heritage, the importance of the waterways, the heyday of the riverboat, and more . . . each panoramic portrait shares a chapter of Paducah's past in highly detailed paintings, whose stories are shared in accompanying bronze interpretive panels.

Take a self-guided tour day or night of these 50 life-size murals, created by world-renowned muralist Robert Dafford, who has created large-scale public works throughout the US as well as in Canada and Europe.

Tip: Stroll Wall to Wall floodwall murals in the evening when the light of the setting sun reflects off the rivers and adds a glow to these magnificent murals.

# Freight House

330 S 3rd St. • 270-908-0006 • freighthousefood.com

✓ Fans of Bravo's *Top Chef* series may be familiar with Chef Sara Bradley and her matzo ball soup, which became a worldwide overnight sensation when she whipped it up during season 16. Everyone who dines at Bradley's farm-to-table restaurant, where the guiding principle is "food is meant to be enjoyed in-season," is in for a treat.

Ingredients for the dishes served here come from the restaurant's own backyard—a backyard that includes berries, bison, and other bounty from mostly Kentucky farms within a day's drive of Paducah—and the food is served in a building that once housed a vegetable depot.

Seasonally changing menus present traditional Southern flavors with a modern twist. You might find griddled meat loaf or Kentucky silver carp cozied up to black-eyed peas or pimento cheese grits. A bonus of an evening at Freight House is the Bourbon Bar, which stocks a staggering selection of bourbons along with a seasonal rotation of cocktails and craft beer.

Freight House (Courtesy of Paducah Convention & Visitors Bureau)

## Nearby Alternatives

### Historic Venue: Hotel Metropolitan

Call to schedule a tour of the first hotel in Paducah operated by and for African Americans. The historic Hotel Metropolitan was listed in the *Green Book* and was part of the "chitlin circuit," which nurtured, welcomed, and gave safe harbor to African American entertainers including Louis Armstrong, Billie Holiday, Ella Fitzgerald, and Duke Ellington during racial segregation.
**724 Oscar Cross Ave., Paducah**
**270-443-7918**
facebook.com/greenbookstop

### Performing Arts Venue: The Carson Center for the Performing Arts

Exemplary staging and near-perfect acoustics are the hallmarks of this state-of-the-art performing arts center designed with space for a wide variety of entertainment, cultural, and education programming—performances by the Paducah Symphony Orchestra, headlining musical acts, splashy Broadway shows, dance performances, dramas, and comedy improv.
**100 Kentucky Ave.**
**270-450-4444**
thecarsoncenter.org

### Outdoors: Wickliffe Mounds State Historic Site

See tools, pottery, and other artifacts used by the Native People of the Mississippian culture in the museum. Browse the gift shop's books, baskets, and jewelry focusing on Native American culture. Explore ceremonial and burial mounds and learn the history of this ancient village located on a bluff overlooking the Mississippi River.
**94 Green St., Wickliffe**
**270-335-3681**
parks.ky.gov

### Outdoors: Columbus-Belmont State Park

Camp cliffside, above the Mississippi River. Hike the Civil War Trail with massive earthen works. See Kentucky's largest Civil War cannon and a section of "Pillow's Folly," the giant chain and anchor that once stretched across the river to fortify the Confederates' position. Also here: museum, mini golf, and snack bar with soft-serve ice cream.
**350 Park Rd., Columbus**
**270-677-2327**
parks.ky.gov

## Trip Planning

### Paducah Convention & Visitors Bureau

**128 Broadway, 800-PADUCAH**
paducah.travel

BENTON
68
KENTUCKY
LAKE
MURRAY
641
INDIA
LLIN
SPER
NON
64
OHIO RIVER
OWENSBORO
FORDSVILLE
54
431
CALHOUN
WAVERLY
41
109
STURGIS
PENNYRILE PARKWAY
NATCHER PARKWAY
GREEN RIVER
81
ROSINE
BEAVER
DAM
WK PARKWAY
PROVIDENCE
TRADEWATER RIVER
109
MARION
MADISONVILLE
CENTRAL CITY
60
GREENVILLE
MORGANTOWN
641
431
WK PARKWAY
CROFTON
BOWLING
GREEN
AH
24
41
24
HOPKINSVILLE
RUSSELVILLE
CADIZ
45
BENTON
68
68
LAKE
BARKLEY
68
LD
41
79
431
FRANKLIN
KENTUCKY
LAKE
OAK GROVE
MURRAY
641
CLARKSVILLE
65
24

# MURRAY

**A**NCHORED BY A HISTORIC downtown court square, Murray is a quintessential small-town college kind of community with lots of heart and very little same old same old. From trendy Shaffer Coffee Co. to Hop Hound Brew Pub, Murray's first microbrewery, and from Bolin Books, with its treasure trove of used, vintage, and rare books, to Red Bug Yarn & Gifts, packed with charm and skeins of yarn, locally owned restaurants and boutiques bring variety and verve to the local landscape.

The "Friendliest Small Town in America" (as Murray was named by Rand McNally and *USA Today*) is also an artistic one. Roam through the Clara M. Eagle Gallery at Murray State University and wander about the Murray Art Guild with its lineup of changing exhibits and Art Market goodies: sculptures, pottery, paintings. Catch a musical at Playhouse in the Park community theater.

Antique lovers are 10 minutes from Hazel, "Kentucky's Antique Capital," and an irresistible jumble of jewelry, glassware, small collectibles, large-scale furniture, old advertising signage, vintage clothing, and more.

# Kentucky Lake

Kentucky Lake Convention & Visitors Bureau
93 Carroll Rd., Benton • 270-527-3128 • visitkylake.com

✓ If warm-weather family vacations conjure up images of sitting side by side with the kids while dropping a line for bass and bluegill; canonballing off the side of a pontoon to see who can make the biggest splash; gathering round a picnic hamper by the shore or grilling dinner as the sun dips into the water; building sandcastles or burying toes; and sharing lots of laughter on sunscreen-scented days—this is Kentucky Lake.

And it's a wonderful time. Wish you were here?

By water: rent a pontoon, fishing boat, kayak or canoe, Jet Skis or tubes from one of the area marinas. Many of the marinas are also resorts offering a variety of lakeview accommodations—lodge and hotel rooms, cottages, and campgrounds.

By land: spend family playtime on a mini-golf course, in an arcade, or at the wheel of a go-kart. Hike or bike a kid-friendly trail. Spoon up a hot fudge sundae from a drive-up diner. Or chill on the beach and enjoy a perfect blue sky lakeside day.

Kentucky Lake (Courtesy of Kentucky Tourism)

Cherokee State Park's dining hall at Kenlake State Resort Park
(Courtesy of Kentucky State Parks)

# Kenlake State Resort Park

542 Kenlake Rd., Hardin • 270-474-2211 • parks.ky.gov

☑ Situated on Kentucky Lake and surrounded by rolling green hills, this hidden beauty of a park surprises with its history, activities, and proximity to nostalgia magnet, the circa-1941 Hitching Post and Old Country Store, stocked with vintage sodas and other cool stuff.

The 300-acre Cherokee State Park—Kentucky's only state park developed for African Americans and the third such park in the United States—opened here in 1951 and brought families from surrounding states to enjoy its beach, cottages, picnic area, dining hall (still in use and listed on the National Register of Historic Places), and other facilities. The park closed in 1963, merging with what is now Kenlake State Resort Park.

Besides state park activity mainstays boating, hiking, fishing, and swimming, Kenlake offers winter indoor tennis (outdoor courts available, too); walking and biking **Eggner's Ferry Bridge**, which spans Kentucky Lake; summer music concerts at the amphitheater; and wintertime self-guided eagle watching. Breakfast is included with overnight stays.

# Rudy's on the Square

104 S 5th St. • 270-917-1207 • facebook.com/rudysonthesquare

☑ Tuck into "meat and three" classic diner comfort food served in one of downtown Murray's most popular gathering places. Serving up charm and Southern homestyle classics in equal portions, Rudy's has been around for eight decades, an icon on the local restaurant scene. As its red awning proudly proclaims, this is "Murray's oldest diner since 1936."

Breakfast is served all day long, and daily specials are tried-and-true faves like chicken livers or gizzards, hamburger steak with gravy and onions, salmon patties, and meat loaf. "Threes" are dishes Grandma made with love and set out on her own supper table: country-style green beans, baked apples, buttered carrots, mashed potatoes, cream corn, tomato relish, cucumbers and onions. And for dessert? Homemade banana pudding, fruit cobbler, and special treat chocolate cobbler.

Slide into one of the red booths inside or grab a sidewalk table outside, sip a sweet tea, and watch the activity on the square.

Rudy's on the Square
(Courtesy of Justin B. Kimbro)

## Nearby Alternatives

### Outdoors: Arboretum at Murray State

Exit the hustle-bustle and enter a sanctuary of wetlands, open prairie and woodlands, grassy plain, and oak and hickory forest. Brimming with native plants, the arboretum is famous for sunsets at "the mountain," where two waterfalls flow into a pond. Visit the **Butterfly Garden**, picnic on the lawn, and . . . breathe.
**300 Hickory Dr., 270-809-3131**
murraystate.edu

### Outdoors: Murray/Calloway County Quilt Trail

With each stitch of the thread, quilt makers share the story of a life, love, or landmark. "The Tree of Life." "Grandmother's Flower Garden." "Hopes and Dreams." More than 60 intricate quilt squares are painted on barns and other buildings on this country trail. See "Double Wedding Ring," splashed on a historic barn and site of the wedding it commemorates.
**Calloway County**
**270-759-2199**
tourmurray.com/
callowaycountybarnquilttrail

### Landmark: Wooldridge Monument at Maplewood Cemetery

This is one for the books (as in *Ripley's Believe It or Not!*):
"The Strange Procession That Never Moves" comprises 18 life-size stone statues—Colonel Henry G. Wooldridge sitting atop his horse, his mother, sisters, brothers, even the family pets—striking a pose in the Maplewood Cemetery in a work commissioned in 1892. TIP: Part of the new Kentucky After Dark Passport Program.
**408 N 6th St., Mayfield**
**270-251-6210**
visitmayfieldgraves.org/
wooldridge-monuments

### Outdoors: Cartwright Grove

Grab your spurs and giddyap into the 1880s and the Wild, Wild West. Tour the saloon, general store, **Billy's Barber Shop**, **Miss Martha's Grand Hotel,** and the little white church, its steeple reaching heavenward. Be wary of Señor Sawbones and behave: the sheriff's office and jail are over yonder.
**Mayfield-Graves County Fairgrounds**
**1004 Housman St., Mayfield**
**270-970-0790**
cartwrightgrove.com

## Trip Planning

**Murray, Kentucky, Convention & Visitors Bureau**
**206 S 4th St.**
**270-759-2199**
tourmurray.com

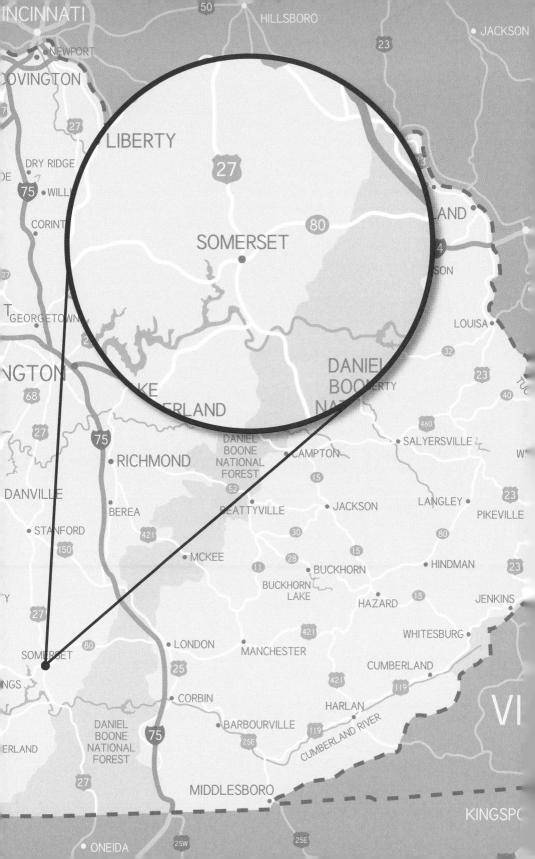

# SOMERSET

**C**IVIL WAR GENERALS, daredevils, vintners, and farmers shape the experiences to be had in this southern Kentucky town in Pulaski County sitting along the northeastern edge of Lake Cumberland.

By land or by lake, there is fun to be had on both sides of the shoreline: rent a houseboat from Burnside Marina or Lee's Ford Resort Marina; hike, swim, camp, bike, fish, and play disc golf at Pulaski County Park; rummage about the pumpkin patch and dart through the corn maze at Bear Wallow Farm; tap into a local craft beer at Jarfly Brewing or Tap on Main.

Browse the Lake Cumberland Farmers Market for everything from fresh produce to wine, soaps, and crafts. Stroll downtown's Fountain Square Park at sunset. Set the kids loose at Miracle Museum, Somerset's irresistibly colorful sensory play park.

Home to the Sheltowee Artisans, a juried art guild that annually hosts two regional art fairs (July and November), and the Master Musicians Festival with marquee entertainers (mid-July), Somerset is also the Car Cruise Capital of Kentucky. Come downtown on the fourth Saturday of the month, April through October, for Somernites Cruise and dozens of classic cars ringing the fountain at the town square.

# Mill Springs Battlefield National Monument

9020 W Hwy. 80, Nancy • 606-636-4045 • nps.gov/misp

☑ "General, it's the enemy." Confederate Captain Henry Fogg to General Felix K. Zollicoffer.

Learn about the key players at the first decisive victory for the Union Army in the Western Theater of the Civil War, which took place on January 19, 1862, on Mill Springs Battlefield.

Watch a film at the visitor center. See the *Combat on the Cumberland* exhibit and its chunk of "Zollie" tree—the large white oak tree beneath which Zollicoffer's body was placed after the Confederate general rode through fog and into a line of Union soldiers. Visit Zollicoffer Park, site of the fiercest fighting, and the Mill Springs National Cemetery.

Take the driving tour through the battlefield. Ten stops include the **Brown-Lanier House**—headquarters for generals on both sides of the fighting; the restored working grist mill; remains of the Confederate field hospital; and Last Stand Hill, where the 17th Tennessee Infantry fought to hold back the federal army so retreating Confederate soldiers could make their escape.

Mill Springs Battlefield National Monument (Courtesy of David Morris)

SomerSplash Waterpark (Courtesy of Lake Cumberland Tourism-SPCCVB)

# SomerSplash Waterpark

1030 KY-2227 • 606-679-7946 • somersplash.com

✓ Zoom 50 feet straight down the speed slide. Slosh and swirl around the bowl slide. Climb 40 feet up before whooshing down one of three body slides and see who makes it to the bottom first. Open Memorial Day through Labor Day, Somersplash is a family magnet with thrill-ride slides, one of Kentucky's largest lazy rivers, and a wave pool with up to four-foot waves, plus spray flowers and water sprays.

A kiddie play area with enormous dumping bucket, play structure with 30 different activities, and wading pool especially designed for smaller children adds to the fun. Chairs and chaise lounges encircle the water zones. Grab some shade beneath an umbrella or rent a private thatched-roof cabana. Bite into burgers, wings, chili dogs, nachos, and other poolside snacks at Tiki's Cantina.

During winter months, the park turns into **Tiki's Winter Wonderland** ice skating rink, with firepits, s'mores, and hot chocolate available.

# Guthrie's Grill

6075 S Hwy. 27 • 606-425-5987 • guthriesgrill.com

☑ Linger over a hand-cut steak with Kentucky bourbon glaze on the patio as the sun slides into beautiful Lake Cumberland. This family-friendly, locally owned American steak house is ever popular with the lake crowd—and for good reason. The restaurant is known for a menu focused on locally sourced ingredients, a staff that genuinely likes to be there, a we're-on-vacation vibe, and those gorgeous lake views framed by surrounding trees.

Besides steaks, chops, and seafood, Guthrie's offers flatbread pizza, pasta, burgers, signature Southern comfort sides like sweet potato casserole, au gratin potatoes, and mac 'n' cheese, as well as a kids' menu and a selection of decadent desserts. Since calories don't count on vacation, bite into the seven-layer white chocolate raspberry cake with house-made fruit puree and buttercream frosting.

The fully stocked bar offers an array of bourbons, and the bartenders know their way around an old-fashioned—dirty martinis, too. Reservations accepted.

Guthrie's Grill (Courtesy of Lake Cumberland Tourism-SPCCVB)

## Nearby Alternatives

### Outdoors: General Burnside Island Golf/General Burnside State Park

This challenging and award-winning course, set on its own island and surrounded by Lake Cumberland, is considered Kentucky's "Best Public Golf Course," according to *Kentucky Living* magazine readers. It is named for Civil War General Ambrose Burnside, who defended the island against Confederate encroachment and whose lavish facial hair spawned the word "sideburns." The park has camping, picnic grounds, a nearby marina, and boat rentals.

**8801 S Hwy. 27, Burnside**
**606-561-4104**
parks.ky.gov

### Outdoors: Big South Fork National River and Recreation Area

Camp, fish, and bike in this backcountry wilderness. Hike to waterfalls and overlooks, double sandstone arches and rock houses, switchbacks and swinging bridges. Spy rhododendron, cliffs, and openings to old coal mines. Hikes range from easy to difficult, the vistas from splendid to spectacular.

**McCreary County**
nps.gov/biso

### Historic Site/Train Excursion: Big South Fork Scenic Railway

Board this vintage mountain train and trundle down 600 feet into the Big South Fork Gorge and Kentucky's logging, coal mining, and railroading past. Explore the Barthell Coal Camp. Pick up a coal miner's lunch. Pop into the **McCreary County Museum** beside the Depot.

**66 Henderson St., Stearns**
**606-376-5330**
bsfsry.com

### Winery: Cave Hill Vineyard & Winery

Come for the gorgeous countryside view; stay for the wine and the vineyard owners' sense of fun. This Kentucky Proud winery prides itself on full-bodied wines that range from dry to sweet. Sample the Naked Lady—one of the winery's most famous labels, made from fragrant pink amaryllis belladonna flowers that grow in Kentucky. (What were you thinking?)

**2115 Smith Ridge Rd., Eubank**
**606-423-3453**
cavehillvineyard.com

## Trip Planning

**Somerset-Pulaski County Convention & Visitors Bureau**
**522 Ogden St.**
**800-642-6287**
lctourism.com

# Index